Inspiration and Elbow Grease

Inspiration and Elbow Grease
Life before Hacks...

Saggy & Moo

This edition published in Great Britain in 2023

Copyright © Sue Price and Maggie Pope 2023

Sue Price and Maggie Pope have asserted their right under the Copyright, Design and Patents Act 1988 to be identified as the authors of this work.

All rights reserved. No parts of this book may be used or reproduced by any means, graphic, electronic, or mechanical, including photocopying, recording, taping or by any information storage retrieval system without the written permission of the copyright holder.

ISBN 979-837-856-004-2 (pbk)

This book is dedicated to

our mother

Joyce Lillian Germaney

who has spent her entire life

looking after other people

About Us

We are actually Maggie and Sue, sisters who were accidentally renamed by an elderly woman with a tendency for spoonerisms. We liked the names so much we decided to keep them.

We were still raising our large families when we eventually went to university in our 40s, Saggy for a BSc [Hons] in Herbal Medicine, and Moo in Psychology. Saggy to build a career as a Medical Herbalist and start a herb school, and Moo just to prove to herself she could not only do it but get a first class degree. Since then she has become far more serious [and good at] photography than psychology.

Contents

Chapter Summaries	xi
Introduction	xiii
1. Making Comparisons	1
2. Making a Home	13
3. Making Food	26
4. Making a Garden	52
5. Making a Plan	66
6. Making an Attempt…	77
7. Making Money Go Round	89
8. Making Memories	101
Where Are We Now?	123
Appendix	125

Chapter Summaries

Introduction

Making Comparisons
In which we look at the way we compare ourselves with others and with our past selves, how one generation compares itself with another, and how we compared our family with the rest of the world.

Making a Home
In which we ask the question why tidy up? We look at the 'art' of laundry, ways to get the kids to clear up after themselves and why this was so important to us.

Making Food
In which we describe school dinners in the 60s, the culinary disasters of our early days as young homemakers, and comment on some tried and tested family favourite recipes. We include a look at how we shopped for food 'back in the day' with memories of the baker's basket brought to the front door and the smelly fishmonger's van.

Making a Garden
In which we describe what Saggy's kids got up to in the garden, and our own childhood dreams of country living on a smallholding. We have fond memories of our Mum's love of gardening but ask if making a garden is worth the effort.

Making a Plan
In which we discover emergency backwards planning, and explain why we maintain we were pioneers of the organisational planner.

Making an Attempt
In which we describe our attempts to raise healthy, kind, hardworking kids. How Saggy applied days of 'restorative medicine' when you weren't fined for keeping kids off school. A chaotic bedtime recalled.

Making the Money Go Round
In which we describe what finances looked like in the 70s and invaluable budgeting advice from our thrifty Grandma Mary. Furnishing a home on a budget, going to auctions and the lengths we went to in saving money. 'Sides to middle' explained…

Making Memories
In which we describe Gravespotting and other rather unusual games our family played, and our Mum's 'Bong Song' bedtime routine which we never forgot. Moo's kids' best fun which she didn't find out about for years, and the time when we were mistaken for a Sunday School outing. A near disaster for Moo's family at sea and how to enjoy going to the dentist. The realisation that our parents didn't behave like normal grandparents.

Introduction

The past is a foreign country: they do things differently there.

L. P. Hartley

Central Heating circa 1968

Who is writing this book?

Two people are writing this book, and our pronouns may get confusing. Sometimes we say *us* and *we*, and sometimes it is *I*

Introduction

and *my*, and sometimes we interrupt each other. We expect our children to know who is who, and what is what. Just persevere, it probably won't make any difference to you.

Why write this book?

We are now in our 60s and wanted to chronicle what our childhood was like, mainly for our kids who do not believe us. Our Mum gave us a lot of freedom which *isn't* always possible today. But she also gave us a lot of fun, which *should* be possible today, with some imagination and flexibility of standards. One massive change has been the influence of social media where homemakers can be manipulated by people sharing opinions about what homes should be like and talking about the best way to organise their kids. This can all bring great pressure on homemakers and parents, whether we want to follow it or not. When we were kids, parents were much freer to do things 'their own way' without comparing themselves too closely with others.

We also wanted to chronicle how we faced the challenge of rearing a large group of kids in the 70s, 80s and 90s

We have to say that home management has evolved since we were married and started our first homes in the 1970s. There were issues we had back then that have disappeared into the mist, but new issues soon popped up to take their place, such as – whose turn is it to load the dishwasher? Some problems seem to have stood the test of time, including the [alleged] fact that men toss their socks in a corner for someone else to pick up and wash and don't know how to use an iron.

Today there are many blogs and YouTube videos advertising the latest life hack to streamline housework and reduce time and effort, but what did we use to do before these hacks were available to make life easier?

Introduction

We have also often been asked how we managed to bring up our families, keep them well fed and adequately – if not fashionably – clothed, pay the bills, run the home on a single income and manage to keep one nostril above the water. It's true we did have to find our way through family life with loads of kids, little money and no idea how to run a home. Well, this is the story of how it went.

Current household management advice books are available, and we can guide you towards them in the spirit of collaboration for the benefit of our nation's homes. And although this book is the culmination of over 80 years of managing a home, it is not all by one person. We share the burden 50/50 with [about] 40 years each, which, we may say, is still ongoing.

The Magic Coffee Table

There was a funny video going the rounds on YouTube about a couple who started to live together. It goes something like this:

Female to male [frustrated]: 'I just wish you'd take some initiative! I work all day, come home, unload and load the dishwasher, make the dinner, do the washing... I can't go on like this.'

Male to female [naively] : 'It will get better, I promise. Come into the kitchen, I've got something to show you. It's a bit of a secret and I'm not sure how it works but – look! There's this basket of dirty washing, and no matter how many times I put dirty clothes in it, somehow next day they are all washed and folded on my bed.'

Female to male [sarcastically]: 'Oh *really*?'

Male to female [with enthusiasm] That's not all! Come into the front room – there's something else. See this coffee table? Well, each night, no matter how much stuff I load it up with, by the next morning it's all gone!

Introduction

Female to male [with attitude]: 'You're insane!'

Male to female [with more enthusiasm]: 'I *know*! I couldn't believe it at first, either! But I've even tested it out, and loaded it up with extra beer cans and dirty glasses, and pizza boxes, just to see how far I can push it, and still the next day it's all gone!

Female to male [walking out the door]: 'I can't deal with this…'

Next Day:

Male to Police Officers [confused]: 'No, she wouldn't *leave* me! What I think happened is this – she got up in the middle of the night to get herself a drink. she tripped over and fell onto the magic coffee table and she disappeared like all my pizza boxes.'

Female police officer [confused]: 'Are you insane?'

Male police officer [bemused]: 'Nah he's telling the truth. I've got a coffee table just like that at home…' [*Credit to* PopcornMax]

We have a problem

By and large whatever type of family we live in, if there is a woman there, she is usually the glue that holds the home and family together. This may not be fair, but it's often the case. When we were kids our Mum had a full-time job after we'd all started school, but she still had to do all the shopping, cooking, washing, ironing and childcare. One could ask 'what did your father do?' which is an understandable question, and it is one we often ask ourselves. The only answer we can come up with is; he read the paper, watched TV, played silly games with our Mad Uncle and generally felt that as he was the man of the house and his job was so responsible, he deserved to relax at home. This may have planted the seed in our souls that *our* kids were going to be taught to help, and *our* husbands were going to take their share of the burden of raising a family. There was a lot of housework

Introduction

and you will find out in these pages how [if] we managed to successfully coerce our young kids into valuable help.

It has been said that it takes at least 37 hours a week to accomplish all domestic work. But this depends on how many people are living in the home, how messy it gets, how big it is and how much of the time people are home. It depends on whether members of the household pursue hobbies within the home that need to constantly be cleaned up, it depends on whether the meals are made from scratch, whether bread is made regularly, whether there needs to be space for mending bikes, doing homework and if there are pets or babies at home.

You might find it necessary to produce something like a written statement. We have produced these many times and found that they help to a certain extent. You can list tasks that need to be done and allocate them to specific people. You can write a timetable so that people know when these tasks need to be done and how often they need to be done. You can then post these statements up in the most visible place in the whole house for people to walk straight past and ignore. There are times when family members have tried to help and tried to follow these timetables, usually when we've discussed them with enthusiasm over a festive evening supper with plenty of chocolate. We sometimes then found that we had many willing hands ready and eager indeed to help for the first day or two.

And yet we have never found that this ran like clockwork without some sort of supervision from us. In the end we found it was quicker to do things ourselves than to chase teenagers to do it, to constantly nag them to do it and then check if they've done it when they've said they've done it. What was most frustrating was that we had friends [mostly abroad] who seemed to have this sussed with no apparent outward effort. Please contact us if you have this one sussed too, although for us it's a bit late…

Introduction

When our children became adults and were still living at home, we thought that we would continue to treat the cooking, the clearing up and the housework as a group, as a team, which is easy to do when you have young children under your control. But, although our children were happy to help, we actually had to *ask* them to help. It wasn't a natural thing for them to assume responsibility for tasks because they started having lives of their own.

So, there it is. We suggest you try to get your family involved, and then have no expectations. If you have expectations therein lies frustration. Make peace with yourself that this is just how it is, and then get on with it…

Chapter 1
Making Comparisons

> *Making Comparisons is a way of thinking about two or more objects, ideas and/or events to find out how they are the same and how they are different. Knowing this information allows [us] to sort, classify and organise objects, ideas and/or events, to connect prior knowledge about them to new knowledge, and to develop appropriate comparative vocabulary...*
>
> letstalkscience.ca

Not a good idea...

It is not healthy to compare ourselves with other people because we usually end up feeling a failure, fatter, scruffier, more stupid, etc. than them. Now we are old we notice that we compare our past with today's way of living, and we tell our kids [and grandkids] about all the ways in which our past was fairer, freer, better morally and less competitive than theirs. We *must stop doing this* as we didn't like it when old people said it to us when we were young. We have also started to compare our present selves with our younger selves, that also is not altogether healthy as we have definitely ended up fatter and slower than we used to be. But it has also made us remember how we used to judge others when we were young, and then compare other families unfavourably with our own – and we consciously kept ourselves a little apart. Did we think we were better? Not sure, but we thought we were different. And we wanted to be different because we wanted to be special:

When you are like everyone, you are nobody; but when you are different from everyone, you are somebody!

Mehmet Murat Ildan

The Past is a Foreign Country

It's hard not to judge the past by the standards of the present because things were done and seen differently. We have to say, even sixty years ago almost seems like a different planet. We have seen a lot of change, mostly gradual, throughout our years, not least in parenting. A lot of it good, and some we're not so sure about.

Us and Them [the generation gap...]

'When *we* were young….' was the beginning of a sentence that we always hated. What followed was always a comparison with what our parents were allowed to do when they were young, with what we wanted to do. Or it preceded a lecture on how much happier/contented/useful/busy/satisfied they were than the 'youth of today'. *They* walked over a mile to see a film at the

Inspiration and Elbow Grease

cinema in the next town because there were no buses and they didn't have a bike, so why were *we* expecting a lift for the half a mile into town? They used to get up at 5.00 am to milk the cows/help their father with the milk round/heat the boiler for the weekly wash, so why did we object to being woken at 7.00 am for school? They had three meals a day and nothing in between, so why did we expect snacks?

I swore to myself that if I ever had kids I would *never* lecture them about what I had to do when I was young. How do you think that went? I would like to suggest that it is almost impossible not to make comparisons between when you were growing up and how one's children view life or want to live. My favourite comparisons when mine were young were in the school holidays and they would complain that there was 'nothing to do'. I could drone on for hours about how I was 'never bored' when I was young. And I think that was true. Especially as I think there was a saying along the lines of, *'Intelligent people are never bored.'*

When we look back on our family life as kids it seems more than one generation away. In the 1950s it was 'de rigueur' for girls to wear pretty dresses, ankle socks, shiny shoes and big bows in their hair even playing in the garden, going shopping or strolling down the road for our mother to show off how neat and tidy we were. Honest to goodness! No elasticated waist jeans, my friend. No easy-wash tee shirts.

There was a time when we were about ten and twelve when our ambition in life was to become nuns. Seriously. This springs from the fact that during the time we were in the church choir one of the young women left to become a nun and she came back (compassionate leave we think) on a visit and *sang in her nun's robes!* How cool was that! So of course, we fancied the dressing up and the utter glory that she got for such a holy life. We hadn't thought through the holy life bit and later we changed our minds (obvs) and decided a much better idea would be to buy a country cottage together and not bother with husbands and children. Just a cat or two on the hearth would be lovely, we thought.

Things couldn't have turned out more wildly different, as it happened. We grew into neat and tidy Grammar School girls, who even wore their brown school blazers over their ordinary dresses *when on a day out with their family*! What craziness is this? Where were our comfy trainers? Where were our hoodies? Even our poor little Squidge of a brother wore his grey primary school blazer. If we had known any better we would have rebelled, but that hadn't been invented yet.

We could make comparisons with discipline from that which we experienced as children, and how then we disciplined our own kids, and how they in turn now discipline theirs. Our parents were rapped hard on the knuckles with a ruler if they wrote with their left hand. When I was nine, I was slapped on the back of the knee by a class teacher because I had pricked my thumb with a needle in sewing class and dropped blood on the cloth.

Moo, Saggy and Squidge were all subjected to the cane from our parents [a thin bamboo cane kept under the kitchen sick. When we tried to hide it a new one would quietly appear]. We smacked our children too when they were young. But when our kids had children, more mercy was being shown to children in general and the naughty step was encouraged. Now it seems that it isn't good even to put a child on the naughty step. Is this what is called Modern Relativism?

With Ourselves [and our past]

Comparison is the death of joy.

Mark Twain

When I was in my 40s, I was late for something and I hustled very fast along the pavement towards our house. One of my daughters [you know who you are...] shrieked with excitement.

'I didn't know you could *run!*' she squealed.

[Exactly the same thing happened to me, only *my* daughter didn't realise ANY mums could run – Moo]

This is what motherhood does to you if you take your eye off the ball. If you have to drive your kids to school instead of walk, if you make several hefty meals a week for teenagers, if you are so tired by the end of the day that you fall asleep while reading a bedtime story to your six year old. I stopped exercising and watching what I ate, and I became sedentary.

But, I would just like to say that I used to be sporty. I can hardly believe it myself. We seem to age so gradually that we barely notice and if we have a family, our attention is elsewhere. My attention was definitely elsewhere, right up until our last child left home when I was 65.

Saggy & Moo

When I was at school, I was deputy games captain in the 3rd year [what is that now, Year 9?]. I played netball and tennis for my House [Romans] and was in the Lower School hockey team [we never lost a match]. I have a wrinkled black and white photo of the team still in my possession which I bring out every single time one of my kids disputes the fact that I have ever played sport. I annotated the photo with a little '*Moi!*' and an arrow over my smug head. I was trying to point myself out in a sophisticated, unassuming way. Like, not boasting or anything, but guys, I'm in the team, see me? Hockey was my game and I loved tearing down the right hand side of the pitch with a well-controlled ball, to whack a clever and perfectly pitched cross to the three forwards who had broken out from the central mass and were rushing towards the goal. Then one of them would stop my pass and in turn whack it into the goal mouth. Go Maidstone Girls' Grammar School third years! This healthy, exercisey little snippet is added to illustrate the fact that I didn't spend all my time studying, playing boarding schools or grave spotting [see Making Memories]. Before sport, I sang in an Anglican church choir with Moo, and for a time, our dear Mum. I have proof of the singing activity too; someone took a photo at the time. I know, a Church choir wasn't X-Factor or anything, but still. We got paid.

Let's face it. We are not going to get our young selves back; but would we want to? We might wistfully remember times when we could actually do sport, yet we find there are a lot of positive when we compare our youth with old[er] age. One of these is *you finally understand who you are and have the confidence to live like it.*

Us and Others [our family v the rest of the world]

Comparisons are odorous.

Much Ado About Nothing

As children we always felt that we didn't come from a normal family, at least compared to any of the other ones we encountered.

Saggy & Moo

Hands up who has a dad that paints lawnmowers purple with a white flower for decoration? Well? And pointing to an upside-down lawnmower to prove what exactly? Why?

Talking of being 'normal', why did he dress up as a Frenchman? We knew of no other family whose father behaved like ours.

Inspiration and Elbow Grease

But if we are comparing families, he didn't come from a totally normal family himself. His father sometimes wore pigtails. Don't tell me that it's because they used to live in Hong Kong. Pigtails weren't mandatory... Goodness knows what it is he was smoking.

Opposite our house was a very sensible family with two well-behaved girls who never laid down in the middle of the road looking at stars when their parents were out like we did. [The risks were small. Our house was in a cul-de-sac]. We couldn't understand why anybody wouldn't find it a thrill to run out of the house late at night, in nighties, always aware that *at any moment* parents could return. We had our ears tuned to the particular sound our car made and we had calculated the exact distance between us and the approaching car that would allow us enough time to dash home and get into bed before being caught.

Further down the road and around the corner was what we called 'bungalow land', which housed either the elderly or the better off. One house contained an older couple who had an only daughter who they treated with smothering, over-protective care. Looking back, who knew the reasons for this? Maybe she had a life-threatening chronic disease, maybe she had been the only child they had managed to bring to term after a series of miscarriages? But when you are young you don't even think about the reasons for things, you just judge. When we saw the poor, white faced girl emerging from her house in the Spring with a winter coat still on and a scarf muffling her face, not to mention a hat with an actual brim, her mother in tow, we just pitied her, glad that our Mum let us roam free on our own with bare faces to the sun. We were once invited to her birthday party and we had never before been in such a clean and tidy house; the overpowering smell was of disinfectant. We were so scared of making a mark on the furniture, or spilling something on the polished wooden floor that we longed to get home to our messy, relaxed home.

We came to realise that most people had tidier homes than we did. One of our neighbours was an Italian lady who had married an Englishman. We were absolutely shocked when we found out that her husband had to take off his shoes when coming home and that she had a pair of 'indoor shoes' that he had to put on instead. So we tried it when we visited, and sure enough she asked us to remove our shoes too. We were gobsmacked. However, she did have this white fur rug in her sitting room which seemed to get marked just by being looked at, so maybe she had good reason. But we knew, with the assurance of youth, that our Mum would have not had the rug if it had placed such restrictions on the family. We compared our homelife with that of our neighbour's kids' and we came off much better, in our opinion. This lady would routinely throw out her kids toys way before they were outgrown, even if they were sentimentally attached to them. We could have understood it if the kids had been teenagers and been hoarding old fluffy bears but these kids were at infant and junior school, and the Mum just didn't want to have clutter around that stopped her cleaning. But once, when I babysat her little kids in her immaculate house, I plumped up the sofa cushions to make them look neat for when she returned. There, under the midnight blue velvety dralon, was the greasy crust of a peanut butter sandwich.

Inspiration and Elbow Grease

When we compared our family to others, we didn't want to be the same. We really, really disliked the idea. When we grew older we wondered why. Why did we sit aloof and not join in the raucous party games with all the other kids? Because the games were silly and childish, is why. Because, if everybody else is doing it, that means we wouldn't. We didn't want to be seen 'joining in' because we had a peculiar sense of snobbery that had no grounding in reality. We lived in a 3-bed semi for goodness sakes, not a mansion. That didn't stop us wandering up and down our cul-de-sac in the evenings when people still had their curtains open and their lights on and peeking in their windows and making comments on how boring their ideas of decoration were and how we were going to create better homes than they had done when we grew up.

The foundation of our childhood seemed to be built on the fact that whatever other people did, we had to do it *differently*.

At this point I must mention that, although *we* didn't live in a mansion, we were friends of kids who *did*. We won't mention their names here but they did live in a proper mansion and had actual *titles*. When the son came to play with Squidge he was caught jumping up and down on our sofa. Our Mum came in and yelled at him to stop [she was no respecter of persons]. Grandma Mary [Dad's mother] was there at the time and she was shocked that our mother could shout at the son of a Lord of the realm. She had great reverence for people with status be they lords, vicars or doctors and would take her apron off just to speak to such beings on the phone. Our Mother just said, 'I don't care who he is, he is not jumping on my sofa.'

When we visited the Lord's daughter at the mansion, we went up the front steps to a grand hall with sweeping staircase. On the left was a huge reception room, which to us looked like Buckingham Palace – they had their sofas grouped in the middle of the room because there was so much space, not pushed against the walls as one has to in a 3-bed semi. We got bored at one point and wandered across the hall to the opposite grand room, and being nosy we opened the door and peeked in. The room was stacked with junk. Rusty bedsteads, old chairs, boxes, cupboards, dirty bikes and books all higgledy-piggledy in piles up to the ceiling. We couldn't make up our minds if this family were posh or just pretending. Anyway, it was here that we had our first taste of home-made ice-cream [which was delicious], so they must have been doing something right.

Many years later, we found out why we distanced ourselves from the common herd. It was genetics. Late in life our father talked to us about how he and his twin [the Mad Uncle] had behaved when they went to birthday parties when they were kids. They refused to sit at the table and eat with the other children. I know! They waited until all the other kids had finished and *then* they got up to the table and ate their tea. *And* they refused to join in all the party games. Why? Because the games were silly and childish, is why. Because if everybody else was doing it, that means they wouldn't. They didn't want to be seen 'joining in'. Because they had a peculiar sense of snobbery that had no grounding in reality. We had no knowledge of this when we were kids, but the apple doesn't fall far from the tree...

Chapter 2
Making a Home

With lots of colour and lots of plants, good smells, plenty of home cooking and loving memories, even a shack can become a wonderful and lovable home

Kate Singh, 'The Homemade Housewife'

What is a home?

Shirley Conran asked this question in her seminal book *Superwoman* [Published by Penguin Books 1977]. She says;

A home is a myth. A home is the Forth Bridge, one damn long, never ending cleaning job, which nobody notices unless you don't do it.

We have to agree that it might feel like this at times, especially if you don't live in a nice house or if you have mice [not as pets], an infestation of cockroaches, damp and mouldy rooms, no heating and awful neighbours. While it is not within our scope to tackle the problems caused by poverty and/or social injustice, we do believe that exercising some control over your environment, creating order, budgeting as best you can and keeping your rooms as clean as you can, will benefit your mental health and make life somewhat easier, if not actually enjoyable.

We think that it is important to run our homes efficiently so we can free time up to do other stuff, hobbies/volunteering/babysitting/walking/cooking etc etc. We who have worked all our lives can fill our spare time with activities that are worthwhile rather than spend our time sitting in front of the TV. And although we can spend our time doing stuff we enjoy, hopefully we can take life at a slower pace, get up later and develop the art of relaxing. Relaxing is much more enjoyable in a clean, well-ordered home.

One more quote from Ms Conran: *You have to be efficient if you are to be lazy...*

What do we mean by home?

So, what were we aiming for in a home? Did we have time and energy to analyse it? Well, actually we did think and talk about it a lot. We researched. We grilled anyone we thought was a

Inspiration and Elbow Grease

successful homemaker. And we learnt. We never stopped learning. We are still learning today.

What we hoped to achieve was a home where everyone felt loved, valued and cared for. Where there was enough good food to eat, a reasonable standard of comfort and order, where there was plenty of fun and laughter. And hopefully enough money to support all that. Luckily, a lot of those things didn't cost much, if anything. Environment is so important, and we instinctively knew that your surroundings impact on your physical and mental health. But how can you achieve attractive homes and pleasant surroundings without spending beyond your means? Fortunately, there are ways you can do this.

People have a much more acute awareness of the importance of creating interiors these days – there are lifestyle TV programmes educating us on how to do it right. We are influenced by influencers and their personal take on candles, bunting, fairy lights and colour schemes. We had none of these when we were young. As to fragrances, there were no plug in aroma diffusers, we went for freshly brewed coffee, newly baked bread, roses from the garden… You might get the odd article in a woman's magazine, but seriously – you did your own thing back then.

We were into a well-stocked bookcase. A house without books did not seem like a home to us. We liked to have plenty of books around. A trip to the library was practically a day out with the kids. They loved lounging on bean bags and looking at books, choosing the ones they liked so they could bring them home and get Mum or Dad to read with them.

As young couples, our first choice when it came to furnishing a home was not Ikea.

As children we used to roam the cul-de-sac where we lived as young teens and shamelessly look into peoples' windows during winter evenings when they had forgotten to pull the curtains.

What we saw was best described as *'conformity'*. It seemed to us that everybody had the same sort of G-plan dining room table and chairs next to a matching sideboard with drinks cabinet and/or bureau, a three-piece suite, a coffee table and a TV on a stand and curtains from the local shopping centre [we recognised them all]. In those days there were only your local shops, or those in the nearest town and everybody in your neighbourhood would buy stuff for their homes from the same places. There was no Internet and therefore no eBay, no Facebook Market Place, no Preloved and no Gumtree. I don't even remember Charity shops. There was, however, the option of looking in your local newspaper under the For Sale column, but it was rare to find enough to furnish your house with.

We swore to ourselves that we would never, ever, make our homes into carbon-copies of other peoples. And we haven't. So far.

Why Tidy Up?

A few of my children live in Scandinavia. Their houses are all easy to clean, well-organised and very, very practical. I can stay with each or any of them for several days and not witness any housework going on, and yet – the houses never seem to get dirty or messy. Well, not *my* kind of dirty and messy. One reason for this may be because, to a man, they all take their shoes off when coming in from outside. This is a practice I have tried to instigate back in the UK, but have, on the whole, been met with a surprised expression of innocence, 'but they're not *dirty*'.

And our houses just aren't made the same. Our houses are much more difficult to clean. We don't have as many cupboards to store stuff in. And we don't usually have separate laundry rooms.

Inspiration and Elbow Grease

None of my kids who live abroad have a washing machine in their kitchen. Not one.

And here we come to the point. There is a special room in the basement of my son's house [a basement so vast, I may add, that it has its own log burner, sauna, washing machine room, drying room and three storage rooms – but I digress] and in this room he has constructed shelves and lined them with containers to, and I quote, 'Finally sort out all the bedding etc'.

When our house was full of children I had serious storage envy, and I know Moo had too. *I* wanted a room lined wall to wall with shelves with containers on to sort my bedding. I loved sorting. Then everything would be at my fingertips when an unexpected guest turned up.

"You want a pillow, or would you prefer two? Certainly, they are in *this* box." A nice fresh-unstained-new quilt would then be extracted from another box. Guest quilt covers would be just above – and oh yes – the pillowcases would be in the box *right above the pillows*. Obviously. Making up a guest bed would have been sheer pleasure. Now the kids have gone I am not sure where the nice clean new quilts or pillows that I had bought especially for guests are. I think my son may have nicked them and put them on his own bed before he left.

And my sheets and covers cupboard? It is in what was the children's bathroom so I suppose I shouldn't be surprised that it is just a muddle because the kids kept opening out folded sheets to see if they were singles or doubles. And they never were the ones that were wanted, and they all seemed to be fitted sheets which were such a pain to re-fold that the kids usually just rolled them in a ball and threw them back in. So, don't come looking in my cupboards is all I can say because I haven't sorted it all out yet. But one day I hope to get a storage system just like my son has.

And this has implications over the whole of the house. Not just bedding. Not just finding a clean pillow for a visitor. Having adequate storage and keeping things in it makes for a tidy home *where you know where everything is* which SAVES OH SO MUCH TIME. This shouldn't be rocket science, but I have wasted hours wondering where the scissors and Sellotape are when I have just 20 minutes to wrap a present before the last post.

As Grandma Mary tried to teach us – a place for everything and everything in its place.

The Art of Laundry: The washing and the putting away

I say putting away because that is where I got stuck. I loved washing clothes, I even loved pegging them out in a gentle breeze on a sunny day. But then I would throw them in a pile somewhere and leave them for a few days as I really dislike

Inspiration and Elbow Grease

folding them up and putting them away. I seemed to be too busy to finish the job. The clothes were clean weren't they? They were dry enough to wear, weren't they? Just smoothing them out and stacking neatly in a cupboard or drawer seemed like a step too far in a life with no hours left in the day for the unnecessary fripperies of neatness.

I know *now* that there are several TikTok videos and books all geared to the problem. I think they are referred to as laundry hacks on how to fold fitted sheets and hoodies neatly. Who knew? Nobody told me how to fold a fitted sheet until I was in my 40s when I stayed in the hospitality wing of a convent when I visited London on the cheap. A nun taught me how to fold a fitted sheet. It took a nun to instruct a housewife how to fold laundry.

When I started married life I had a twin tub [1975]. These were big machines that you could wheel out from under a countertop [usually hidden by a gingham curtain] and fill with water from a hose attached to your kitchen sink tap. One half was the washer; this was the half you filled with water, and the other half was a spin drier. After you put the right amount of water in and added the powder you would close the lid and switch on the heater to get to the right temperature. Then you would add the whites and set the timer, as this was your first load. You would have 3–4 loads waiting and they all got washed in the same water – hence you wouldn't start with the darks or muddy outdoor clothes. After the whites were done you would hoik them out with vast wooden tongs and slop them over to the spinning side. You would want to try and squeeze as much water as possible out of them as they transferred across because:

- you didn't want to empty the washing side of too much water, and:

- you would try to make the spinning side as quick as possible by reducing the quantity of water going in with the clothes.

The art of loading the spinning side was to coil the garments or sheets around the outside wall of the spinner. If you just plonked them in willy-nilly the spinning would make an awful banging racket that sounded like the spinner was about to break. You would always have to remember to hook the hose which took the soapy water out of the spin side back into the tub, so you didn't waste it down the drain and then, as you hosed in clean water to rinse the clothes [with yet another hose] you would hook the first hose over the kitchen sink. You would have to rinse, spin and repeat until the water ran clear into the sink with no soap suds. Then you would remove the washing from the spinner, shake and hang. As the washing was still very damp when it came out of the spinner it was hung outside to dry in the elements if humanly possible [i.e. not raining] or it would have to be hung on a wooden clothes horse in front of the fire. Just as people do now if they have no tumble drier in the damp, cold winter.

Moo started married life with a copper boiler and a mangle in Army quarters [1973]. You would actually have to light the gas under it to heat the water. The mangle had rubber rollers; she said it was the 'modern type, not like the wooden mangle that Grandma Ruth [Mum's mother] had'. Excuse me, a *modern* mangle? She then inherited our Mum's twin tub soon after the copper boiler. Then, when she upgraded to an automatic, I got the twin tub. By the time I upgraded to an automatic that sturdy twin tub had been going strong for over 20 years…

But spare a thought for the mums of the 50s [actually, make that up to and including the 80s]. No disposable nappies for them; nappies were cloth squares made up of a white towelling material which was soft and absorbent but were not thrown away.

Inspiration and Elbow Grease

They had to be washed. Mums were lucky if they had a washing machine. This is what they had to do with nappies;

∽

'Wet napkins should be put in a covered pail of water, dirty napkins into another pail with disinfectant. The wet ones should be washed, rinsed and hung up to dry. Dirty ones are shaken over the W.C.' [to roll the solids off...] 'scrubbed under the tap with a hard brush and soap, left soaking for some time in cold water and washed out in a good lather with soap or soap flakes. Rinse them thoroughly in several changes of clean water, then dry them and let them air thoroughly. If you can, have a proper wash tub in the scullery and wash the napkins there. Leaning over a bath is back-breaking work...' From *The Care of Young Babies* 1940.

∽

When I had kids of a reasonable age, I put one kid in charge of the washing. I taught a couple of them the principles of sorting washing into piles of whites, darks, woollens, etc. I had a landing wide enough to house a section of racking on which I placed a named plastic basket for each child. All the kid with the washing basket had to do was to place the basket of dry, clean washing on the landing and fold each item carefully and place in the relevant basket. This worked a treat.

One of my sons joined the Navy and soon learned to iron better than I ever could. I had originally tried to foist the job on one of the girls and had even bought her her own special iron. We called her Tiggy [after Mrs Tiggy-Winkle, the hedgehog who ironed, in a Beatrix Potter story] but the experiment wasn't a long-term success.

Saggy & Moo

There are TV programmes now on how to completely reorganise your home [like Sort Your Life Out on BBC], but in the 1980s what was there? Well, I don't know because we didn't get a TV till about 2011... But books? We remember avidly reading Don Aslett's *Is There Life After Housework* [1982], and also his *How to Win at Housework* [1983]. He made this promise about his first book:

'A revolutionary approach to free you from the drudgery of housework'.

One of the reasons that we liked this book was a sentence in his housework manifesto: *You are entitled to a life of love, fulfilment and accomplishment, but you will find these rewards almost impossible to obtain if you spend your life thrashing and wallowing in a muddle of housework.*

One big benefit to keeping the house tidy is that it is easier to clean. I now employ a cleaner just once a week, but I still tidy up before she comes as we pay her to clean, not pick up my husband's clothes off the floor before she vacuums. When all my kids were at home there is no way we could have afforded a cleaner, but it was my firm conviction that children should learn to clean their own rooms and to tidy up after themselves. I remember buying my kids their own personal buckets and cleaning cloths and sending them on cleaning missions around the house. I used to do this a lot in the holidays because there was plenty of time to fill, and why should they lay in bed till midday while I am tidying up after them? However, usually we needed to give our kids a metaphorical carrot. Which brings us to Saturday Special...

Saturday Special and the List

I may have come across as a crotchety type of housewife, who nagged at her kids to help around the home. The reason I did this was, not [just] because I didn't think it was fair leaving the work to the mother because she was the housewife while the kids did as they pleased with some sort of 'entitlement'. But, because I felt it was good for their future if they knew how to clean up after themselves and be independent.

Most of this feeling was developed in us both at a very young age because we watched our mother being treated like a general dogsbody even though she also worked. Our father was of the generation that left all the housework and cooking to 'the wife' while the husband would come home from work, sit in his armchair with the newspaper and wait to be called to the table for his dinner. Our Mum would have come in from work about an hour before Dad but in that time would have had to take off her coat as she was peeling the potatoes and wash up the breakfast things left by us kids before school. What were we doing?

We would come home, dropping coats and bags on the floor, make a snack, shove the plates in the cold washing up water [where our breakfast dishes still were] and go and do our homework. Or read. Or play in the street. Not once do we remember thinking we might help our Mum by washing up the breakfast things.

After dinner, everybody would wander off leaving our Mum to clear the table, wash up, dry up and then do stuff like iron our Dad's shirts or put on a wash. Just as she would be thinking of sitting down with the rest of us, our Dad would say. 'What's for supper?'

So, it doesn't take much imagination to understand why we were so determined not to let our kids grow up like us...

Practically speaking it wasn't always easy. But I did develop one very clear strategy from when they were small. I not only felt that kids should help around the house from a young age, I also felt that they shouldn't eat too many sweets and I combined these two strategies in something I christened Saturday Special.

My approach was this. I would totally keep them off sweets for the whole week until Saturday. I would buy a very nice sweet selection along the lines of Pic n' Mix on the Friday afternoon and a comic each. Saturday morning I would write each child a list of jobs. I started to draw these lists for the kids who couldn't read and ended up illustrating each individual list for each child. The lists would go something like this:

1. Help clear breakfast
2. Brush teeth and make bed
3. Tidy bedroom
4. Hang washing on line
5. Vacuum front room
6. Unload dishwasher

Inspiration and Elbow Grease

7. Wash downstairs windows
8. Mop kitchen floor
9. Put washing away
10. Make bread dough
11. Mow lawn
12. Peel potatoes
13. Dust front room and playroom
14. Clean the bathroom

No child got all the above jobs, obviously. I mentally sorted through what needed doing and divvied up the jobs accordingly. By lunch time the lists were usually finished and we had lunch. After lunch I brought out plastic beakers and dished out sweets into each cup. I sent all the kids to their rooms with a cup of sweets and a comic with the instructions that they were *not allowed out of their rooms for at least an hour.* They had to lie on their beds, eat sweets and read a comic for an hour. They didn't have to sleep, but some usually nodded off.

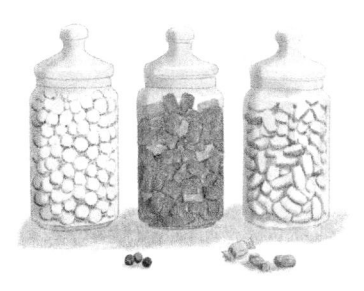

One big advantage to this was that I got at least an hour with a cup of tea and a biscuit in complete peace with my feet up in a clean and tidy house.

Moo also had a similar approach but not as well organised [her comment, not mine].

Chapter 3
Making Food

'Paupers, my mother crisply observed, cannot afford to be squeamish, and she has a point'

Jocasta Innes, 1971

Tales of deprivation

We were brought up on horror stories of our mother's childhood diet. We might have thought we needed to be careful with money, but not many people could be more 'careful' than our maternal grandma.

Mum still regales us with tales of deprivation which were unusual even in 1930s and 40s Britain. A favourite one is the single spoonful of boiled egg dished out to each child on a slice of bread and margarine for their tea. Meat was a luxury only enjoyed once a week by their father; any leftovers went into his sandwiches. The kids were thankful for the gravy and were lucky that there was an allotment which provided them with vegetables.

It's hard to believe, but Grandma Ruth used to 'roast' potatoes in water. Mashed potato was watery and sloppy and was splatted onto dinner plates in a most unappetising way. Grandma might occasionally treat herself to a packet of crisps, but a child would only be offered one crisp each if they were lucky.

Maybe the worst thing was that Grandma Ruth would sell the children's food rations during and after the war to pay off what she owed on her 'book', that is, clothes she was buying herself on credit. Not surprisingly, this still rankles with mum nearly ninety years on...

Our childhood diet

In the 1950s and 1960s our diet, like most other people's, was quite plain. Home cooked, heavy on the carbs, nothing exotic. We enjoyed Mum's cooking, which is just as well because we had no say in what was on the menu. Uppermost in Mum's mind was cooking to please Dad and making sure we never went hungry like she had done as a child. Dad would often be fed ox hearts and kidneys while we were happy to have sausages. Of course, there was a roast dinner every Sunday with expertly crisped up potatoes, perfectly turned out Yorkshire puddings and smooth rich gravy.

Puddings [we called them 'afters'] included apple pie, suet pudding, jam roly poly, treacle [syrup] tart, tinned fruit or bananas with evaporated milk.

Mum did her own baking. How good to come home from school to the smell of coconut buns just out of the oven! They were crisp on the outside and soft and meltingly delicious on the inside and heavenly when eaten whilst still hot. Apple pies, tarts, cakes, buns, mince pies – all were made by Mum. Then there was the mixing bowl to be scraped out, all three of us trying to get a share of the remains of the cake mixture at the same time…

Looking at photos of us as young children we are surprised at how skinny we were.

Until we were adults, we had never tasted garlic, fresh herbs [apart from mint], pizza or any foreign cuisine whatsoever.

School Dinners

At Grammar school we were served hot school dinners in the refectory [a posh name for a collection of large wooden huts by the pottery classrooms]. The choice was very traditional: eat it or go hungry. One day every week we were given liver and bacon. I have always found liver very dry, but at least it was served in a watery but tasteless gravy, and a mound of mashed potato. The skill was to insert a cube of liver into a forkful of mashed potato and try not to remember it was there but to chew and swallow quickly. Can you imagine serving liver to today's secondary school pupils? Can you imagine them eating it? I suppose it was served because it was very cheap and very nutri-

Inspiration and Elbow Grease

tious; it would supply the pupils with a daily quota of protein and B vitamins.

Moo and I had been primed to eat what was put in front of us by going through the Primary school system with Mrs Cecil. Mrs Cecil was a dinner lady, and these women appeared every meal time in their white coats and funny hats pushing a trolley to each classroom. We ate our dinners at our desks and were watched while doing so. I strongly objected to Gypsy Tart [didn't we all? – Moo] which was a form of dessert – a sweet pastry base with a filling. This filling was my Waterloo, my Nemesis. The filling was a whipped, sticky goo that tasted like very, very sweet butterscotch with a hint of coffee. The sauce it was served with was also something whipped up to a froth and had a funny taste.

One day I refused to eat it.

Mrs. Cecil stood over me, arms folded across her ample bosom, while she supervised me eating Every. Last. Mouthful. This meal had been paid for and, by God, it was going to be consumed. She had a smirk of triumph when she at last reached over to collect my empty bowl. What happened next was purely out of my control, but it was timed to perfection. As she stood up with my dish I bent forward and vomited up the whole meal, sauce and all, over her polished shoes.

I think she cuffed my ear as if she felt it was deliberate. I most certainly was not given any sympathy for being unwell but chastised for wasting what she termed 'good food'.

At least I had the good sense to reject refined flour and sugar and not protein and B vitamins…

At primary school we were also given milk at morning playtime. This came in dinky little bottles and was drunk with a paper straw. It was always too warm in summer when you wanted a cold drink and freezing cold in winter when you needed a hot drink to warm you up. For a penny you could buy a biscuit to go with it and for twopence a big fancy wafer biscuit. Nobody was expected to have a milk allergy; it was rare in those days.

The Early Days

Mistakes were made...

Mistakes cannot really be avoided when you set up home for the first time and are suddenly responsible for cooking your own meals. In our youth there was no 'Deliveroo' or similar, and the only take away we ever saw was Fish and Chips. In reality any take away options, or ready meals, were too expensive for us [I had just left school at 18 and had deferred Uni for a year while husband was still at college.] So we were skint. I had had no real experience of *cooking* as my Mum made such good dinners, and no experience of *budgeting* as Mum just seemed to do it without planning. So I had to suddenly cook from scratch with very little money and even less know-how.

I had heard that tripe was a nutritious and cheap dish, so I went to the butcher and bought some tripe. It was indeed very cheap – it cost mere pennies. Tripe, my friends, is the first or second stomach of a cow or other ruminant used as food. I am not sure you can even buy it now, with good reason – mainly because it looks disgusting.

I had an old cookbook which had a recipe for preparing tripe and I followed it to the letter. The book was a 1947 edition of *Cookery Recipes – Household Cookery and Economy Supplement* from the Battersea Polytechnic Domestic Science Department, and it said:

Ingredients:

- 1lb of tripe
- 2 large onions

Inspiration and Elbow Grease

- ¼ pint milk
- ¾ pint water
- 1 tablespoon water
- 1oz flour
- salt and pepper

1. Peel the onions and leave whole. Blanch tripe and cut into neat pieces.
2. Return to saucepan, with onions, salt, water. Simmer 2 hours. Remove onions, chop them.
3. Mix the flour to a smooth paste with a little cold milk.
4. Stir the paste into the tripe and onions, and the seasoning. Boil 5 minutes and serve garnished with chopped parsley.

When my unsuspecting husband cycled home from college, he had no idea of the Tripe Treat that awaited him. I got it out of the cooker with housewifely pride and set the lordly dish before him. I served up a handsome portion each and we took one mouthful. I would have to say that another reason for it not being widely on sale today is that it tastes as disgusting as it looks. Hungry and poor as we were, our meal that night was thrown in the bin and we feasted on sliced white bread, spread with cooking margarine and topped with cheap supermarket jam.

One of our wedding presents was a pressure cooker. This was supposed to save us time and money by cooking cheap cuts of meat quickly, and to cook several vegetables at the same time in little inserts within the cooker all on the same gas ring. And I am sure it *would* have been able to do these things; so sure am I of the economic efficiency of a pressure cooker that I am contemplating getting a modern one even now. However, at 18 I knew nothing about the mechanics or working philosophy of a pressure cooker, I just opened the page on timings for cooking chopped steak for a stew and went to the shops. Now, here was the error. I went to the *shops* not the *butcher*. If I had rocked up at the local butcher this sorry tale may have had a more positive ending. However, in the shop there were tins of stewing steak. Stewing steak! Just what I needed. So I bought two tins, went home, tipped the meat and gravy into the pressure cooker, checked the timings and set the equipment off. I was a little scared of the hissing, rattling and steam escapage from the weights at the top but, having double checked the timings, I was confident all was well, although I did take the cautionary act of hiding in the dining room with a book until the timer had gone.

With great excitement, I followed the instructions for opening etc, only to find a black mass stuck fast the the bottom and sides of the cooker. I could also smell burning. This black mass was all that was left of the meat that was supposed to be our stew. What had gone wrong? It took my husband to explain to me that the recipe called for uncooked meat, which the pressure cooker was supposed to cook. A pressure cooker was not for already cooked and seasoned meat [in gravy] from a tin that just needed a warm through in a saucepan. I never used a pressure cooker again. Partly through fear of explosions, but also from embarrassment.

I am a Frenchman. I cannot eat a meal without bread. Andre L Simon

---

I had an interesting bread making journey. As a new housewife one of my aims was to make fresh bread. I had been enthused by a tiny brown booklet by Elizabeth David which my husband had bought me in 1973 while I was still at school studying for my O-levels [he wasn't my husband then of course, obviously, just wanted to be absolutely clear...]. Mrs David's diatribe against the English and their bread both lit a fire of wanting good bread

Inspiration and Elbow Grease

and shame that we as a nation had stooped so low that we couldn't even have good bread on sale in our shops. We could not, even as customers, learn to discern and demand it. We were just too accepting of bad food. I was going to join her mission to improve the nation's bread, starting with ours.

The booklet was called *The Baking of an English Loaf*, and it had cost 15p and started with a quote from Eliza Acton [The English Bread Book 1857]: *A very exaggerated idea of the difficulty and trouble of breadmaking prevails amongst persons who are entirely ignorant of the process.*

Elizabeth David adds: 'Any human being possessed of sufficient gumption to track down a source of fresh yeast -it isn't all that rare- and collected enough to remember to buy at the same time a pound or two of plain flour, get it home, take a mixing bowl and a measuring jug from the cupboard, and read a few simple instructions can make a decent loaf of bread. And if you cannot, after two or three attempts, make a *better* loaf than any to be bought in an English shop – and that goes for health-food and whole-food and crank-food and home-spun shops generally, just as much as for chain bakeries and provision stores and small independent bakers – then I am prepared to eat my hat, your hat, and almost anything put before me, always and with the absolute exception of a loaf of English commercial bread.'

Although I make really great bread now, the comment from Mrs David about 'two or three attempts' was very accurate. My first attempt was shortly after I got married and is best forgotten. I bought the wrong type of flour for a start, but it was my *method* of working that I remember so clearly and which is not very easy to explain logically. Most people know that bread dough can take over an hour to double in size, ready to be shaped into loaves. What do people do in that hour? Some may clear the kitchen, sweep the floor, make the beds or pop to the shops. Not me. I took this breadmaking adventure seriously. When it said one had to wait for the dough to rise, I waited. I did nothing else. I brought a book into the kitchen and sat next to the rising dough, watching and waiting. It was as if my very presence next to the bowl would somehow cause the dough to rise with due diligence and not disappoint me. I did this watching and waiting malarkey for some years before the penny dropped that I could actually leave the dough to do its own thing without being babysat.

Even capable Moo had her rite of passage into the food-making-file-of-failures.

As she says: Early days of being a very young housewife were fraught with anxieties and a desperate desire to prove I knew what I was doing. I didn't. My biggest worry was how to produce the perfect roast dinner. This was my biggest worry because my husband was a meat and three veg eater whose own mother had cooked a roast each Sunday for their big family. It was something that he expected to be carried on by his own wife. The thing was, his mother had never made it look like it was much effort at all and she had done it so often. No pressure then. I hadn't even helped my own mother make our roast dinners. The most I had learnt was how to make mint sauce from watching Dad mix chopped mint from the garden with malt vinegar. This represented his total contribution to cooking, by the way. I knew how to do *this* because I had helped him pick the mint. But cook the meat to be tender not dry, at the same time as crisping up the roast potatoes so they are not soggy? No.

~

The first time I attempted it I put on a confident front, but inside I was nervous. It was like the ultimate housewifery exam, which I was about to take with no preparation at all. For a start, I couldn't tell chicken meat from chicken fat. [Seriously? Even I knew that – Saggy]. I had never looked at raw chicken before and

Inspiration and Elbow Grease

thought that pale stuff must be all fat. Well, I had to cook it anyway and see how it went. Somehow it wasn't too bad, although I hadn't a clue how to time the vegetables to be ready exactly on cue.

And then there was the gravy. In my husband's childhood home, the gravy made the meal and of course, our Mum's gravy was always perfect. So, the quality of the gravy was the final test. I knew Mum always used Bisto to thicken the meat juices and veg water. But what I *didn't* realise was that you have to mix it with *cold* water before you add it, so I just tipped a load of powder into the hot veg water. Even if you don't study Physics, I expect you know what I seem to have overlooked. Powder thrown en masse into hot fluid forms lumps.

The gravy was a mess. It was a thin brown fluid with solid lumps of Bisto powder floating on the surface. This was, as far as I was concerned, a complete disaster. I had failed. The problem was that instead of sympathising with my grief, my husband didn't see it as quite the worst thing that had ever happened. He laughed – not *at* me, but as an attempt to jolly me out of my despair. Did I see the funny side and laugh it off? No, I did not. I got angry about failing and was hurt for being laughed at. I performed the usual attempt people make at an exit when embarrassed. I flounced out of the room. I slammed the glass door of the dining room behind me.

The sound of breaking glass cascading on the floor made me turn round just in time to see my husband's arm appearing through the glass. Had he tried to come after me to comfort me? I never found out in the rush to mop up blood and get to A&E. I was mortified, but I have to say I am good at flouncing. [Me too – Saggy]. There was to be a repeat of the arm through the glass scenario many years later, but that's another story…

35

Thank goodness we came across *The Pauper's Cookbook*. How would we have managed without it? First published in 1971, Jocasta Innes says in the introduction that she had been waiting for someone to write a book like this, one geared to the tastes and limitations of a greedy pauper. This seemed to be the category that best described us so, each armed with a copy, we launched ourselves wholeheartedly into a career of getting the best results from the least amount of money.

Or, as she succinctly put it, to be *'thrifty without appearing stingy'*.

There was a time early on, before Jocasta Innes stepped in to guide us, when our two families lived together. It was just for six months but expenses were high and income was low. We had to feed four adults, one small child and a baby on as little as we could get away with. In the very early days, we discovered *Modern Vegetarian Cookery* by Walter and Jenny Fliess. Meat free meals seemed like a good idea because meat was out of our price range, except maybe for mince and offal. Happy memories of Baked Savoury Roll! – Stewed chopped veg, mushrooms, herbs and nuts with yeast extract all wrapped up in pastry. Although to be honest, I only remember the mushrooms and yeast extract. It was delicious [and cheap] anyway.

It was all so much simpler in the beginning.

Meal Planning

Planning ahead what to eat is the cornerstone of thriftiness in the kitchen. It makes so much sense and seems so obvious that we have been surprised to find that it isn't done in every household where money is tight. That, and learning basic cooking skills, is the basis of managing the food bills. Having said that, it wasn't so obvious to us when we were young mums and that is where *The Pauper's Cookbook* came into it. It helped us lay a good foundation for the years ahead.

Inspiration and Elbow Grease

Meal planning was the first lesson.

So, once a week we would come up with a menu for the week ahead. It didn't occur to us to ask the children what they wanted. After all, nobody had ever asked *us* what we fancied when we were children. We couldn't afford to pander to individual preferences anyway. As the person in charge of our children's health AND the household budget we did our best to get as much bang for our buck, nutritionally speaking, as possible. That meant drawing up a weekly menu, deciding what would be needed to cook it, checking what was already in the cupboard, writing a shopping list and pretty much sticking to it. This also limited the number of times we had to go shopping and get tempted to spend.

There was no alternative to what we dished up, except that you either ate it or you didn't. I suppose when you think about it, we were very lucky not to have had a vast array of convenience foods available to us at the time, so at least that wasn't an option. That's not to say we didn't have any picky eaters, but they were in the minority and never starved. Pickiness was kept to a minimum by lack of options and not making a battle out of mealtimes.

The best laid plans…

Programmed Eating

Programmed eating was something we learnt from *The Pauper's Cookbook* and was foundational to thrifty budgeting. The idea was to build the week's meals around a big, relatively expensive item like a chicken. Something that would be the basis for three meals minimum. A week's menu might go something like this:

Day 1. Roast chicken
Day 2. Chicken Leftovers

Day 3. Chicken Stew
Day 4. Baked Savoury Roll
Day 5. Alsatian Onion Tart
Day 6. Onion, bacon and potato hotpot
Day 7. Lentil Rissoles

Once the chicken was cooked and every scrap of meat taken off the carcass, the bones would be boiled up for stock which was the basis for a stew or soup.

Programmed eating not only saved money but time as well, which was also in short supply. When you know in advance what you will be cooking, it saves a lot of last-minute hassle.

The Cheap Week

Fairly frequently our funds were *very* low. There were no foodbanks back then, so at times like these we would embrace what we termed a 'cheap week'. This meant that we would scrape through the week buying nothing but sheer necessities, and even then eating the most basic, low cost meals we could find. Some of these we have included in Making Food. Far from this being a gruesome chore, I quite enjoyed it [Saggy]. I found it a challenge so I could brag about how little I'd spent [Moo].

Anyway, both lots of families regularly took on this challenge on with gusto and came up with some very interesting meal suggestions. Refined carbohydrates obviously featured large as these were very cheap and filled a child up without straining the purse strings over much. We didn't know *how bad* they were then; we were more concerned with making sure our kids were not hungry. Perhaps we were so determined not to give our kids the same experience our mother had had – at least we could stretch to a whole egg each as long as the toast wasn't organic stone ground spelt which needed a loan to buy enough for a week's sandwiches.

No, even when we made our own bread it was plain old cheap refined flour from the supermarket, not from a local artisan mill. In the end our kids' health doesn't seem to have been impacted badly, and I stoutly claim it was because we cooked from scratch and didn't buy ultra-processed foods, coca cola or packet mixes impregnated with MSG and microwave meals.

Family Favourites

We soon found there were family favourites. Standard dishes, cooked from scratch, that we liked to return to often because they were filling and cheap:

Bacon rice – based on a recipe gleaned from a West Indian friend many years ago. Her version included half a chicken cooked in butter with bacon, onions, sweetcorn and tomatoes and seasoned with celery seeds. Our version was cheaper because we usually left out the chicken and just had bacon pieces, but we did sometimes include mushrooms as well. You just sauté chopped bacon and onions in some fat in a deep thick pan, when onions are glazed then add basmati rice and sauté a bit more, then add some water, a tin of chopped tomatoes and a tin of sweet corn. A tsp of sugar takes away the tinned taste of the tomatoes. Add salt and pepper, but the MAIN CONDIMENT IS CELERY SEED – this is what gives the dish its unique taste. Trust me. Though if you can't get celery seed then get celery salt at a pinch. This was a recipe that was passed down orally, so has no real quantities…

Onion, bacon and potato hotpot – this was a delectable [and very cheap] dish consisting of layers of potatoes, onions and bacon covered in a white sauce and cooked for what seemed like forever. It smelt and tasted divine! However, it was a bit of a fiddle and not something you could knock up in a hurry. This led to a crushing comment from a visiting family member when one of us, being extremely strapped for cash and having lots of mouths to feed, went to the trouble of cooking this lovely meal for her visitor. The visitor expressed her disappointment with the meal. "When I have visitors, I make an effort!" Perhaps she had roast beef or leg of lamb in mind, neither of which were ever seen on our dining tables as far as I can remember.

Baked Savoury Roll For 4. Short pastry from ½lb flour, 4oz butter and 4 tbs water. *Filling:* ¼ small cabbage/1 onion/2 carrots/1 leek/1 tomato/A few mushrooms/1 tsp mixed herbs/1 oz fat/1 tsp yeast extract/1 tsp flour or cornflour/1 oz grated nuts/½ egg.

Chop or mince all the vegetables finely. Melt the fat in a saucepan and stew the minced vegetables in it for about 10 minutes, stirring from time to time. Take it off the flame and add the nuts, herbs, yeast extract and add flour. Mix well and cool. Roll the pastry out into a large square about ⅛ inch thick and spread the minced vegetable mixture evenly over it. Leave the edges free and paint them with the whisked raw egg. Then roll up the pastry with the vegetables, fold the sides over and press them down. Paint the top and sides with egg and, if desired, sprinkle a little salt on top. Bake in a hot oven (400–425F, gas 6 or 7) for 30 to 40 mins or until the top is brown. Serve with gravy.

Pork and beans – another one we got from the good old *Pauper's Cookbook.* Slices of belly pork chopped and cooked with beans and molasses. It was light on the pork and heavy on the beans, very *Little House on the Prairie,* very tasty, very cheap, very popular.

[4–6 helpings] 1lb dried haricot beans, ½lb streaky pork, 1 large onion, dash of Worcestershire sauce, 2 tbs black treacle [molasses], 1 dessertspoon brown sugar, 1 dessertspoon mustard powder, salt & pepper. Soak the beans overnight. Cook for 1½–2 hours in the water they were soaked in. Strain and keep the

Inspiration and Elbow Grease

water. Cut the pork into chunks, removing rind. Peel and slice onion. Heat the bean water and stir in the treacle, Worcestershire sauce, mustard, sugar, salt and pepper. Mix up the beans, pork and onion in a casserole, pour over the bean water [adding more hot water if necessary to cover the beans]. Cover and bake in a moderate oven [gas 4, 350F, 180C] for about an hour, or until the beans are soft. If the beans are dry while cooking add a bit more water. This is a rich sweetish dish and goes best with an uncloying vegetable like spring greens.

Lentil rissoles – this came from *Modern Vegetarian Cookery*. Well, the basic recipe did. It has been through many variations, and we are still making lentil rissoles today. Just cook red lentils till mushy, and drain. Add an egg when cooled and a handful of rolled oats. Meanwhile, fry chopped onions and mushrooms with plenty of spicy stuff [like chillies, cumin, turmeric, garlic etc – otherwise these will be very bland] and salt and pepper. Mix with lentils and form into shapes, then fry in coconut oil.

Autumn vegetable casserole – I can't remember where this one came from, possibly a magazine. It was a casserole of vegetables, as you might expect, but with a cheesy dumpling sort of topping. Absolutely gorgeous...

Alsatian Onion Tart [*Pauper's Cookbook*] – All you need is pastry, lots of onions, butter and a couple of eggs. It's surprisingly tasty.

Line flan tin with short crust pastry. Peel and chop 2lbs onions [you can make do with less] and cook them over a low heat with just enough water in the pan to stop them burning. When they are soft and tender, add a generous lump of butter and leave to stew a few minutes longer. Then take them off the heat and add just enough flour to bind them. [1–2 tablespoons], salt, black pepper, 2 beaten eggs and, if possible, 1 tablespoon of cream or the top of the milk, to make a thick mush. Spread this onion mixture in the flan tin, spoon a little more cream [grated cheese could be used] over the top and bake in a fairly hot oven [gas 7, 425F, 220C] for 20 minutes, then lower the heat a couple of notches and continue cooking till the pastry is crisp and the top nicely browned, ¾–1 hour. A plain green salad goes well with this. No other vegetables.

To line one 8–9 inch flan case you will need:

6oz plain flour, 3½oz butter [chilled], 1 egg yolk, 1–2 tablespoons water, pinch salt, squeeze lemon juice.

1. Sift flour and salt together into a large mixing bowl.
2. Make a well in the centre. Put in the butter and start cutting it into the flour with a knife. The idea is to break the butter up small while working in as much flour as possible. When the knife seems to have done what it can, use your fingertips to rub the mixture together till the butter has absorbed all the loose flour and the particles are the size of fresh breadcrumbs. *Don't* overdo this stage to be on the safe side – pastry is better handled too little than too much.
3. Beat up the egg yolk with the water and stir into the crumbs with your knife. Add a squeeze of lemon juice to make the dough more pliable.
4. Gather the sticky mess together with your fingertips and work lightly till it sticks together in a lump and some of the stickiness has gone.

Rest in a cool place for an hour or so before use. The point of this is to make the dough less tough and less liable to shrink in cooking.

To roll the dough out, flour the table top and the rolling pin and dust a little flour over the lump of pastry itself if it feels very sticky. Roll out lightly but firmly and lay over the flan tin, press down firmly once in place.

Food Shopping

Perhaps one of the biggest differences between family life now and 'back in the day' is the way shopping was done. A lot of time could be spent on food shopping and not in a good way. Some housewives in the 50s and 60s still shopped daily for fresh food and, while this could be seen as an indulgence, like the French, the truth was more prosaic. Housewives had to shop daily because they didn't have freezers or, in some cases even then, fridges. And they could only buy what they could carry home, as it was not common for all families to have a car and even if they did it was for the 'man of the house'. Lots of mums didn't drive; it was thought by some to be *too complicated* for them. Our mother never learnt to drive even after we got a car in 1964. She knew very well that if she learnt to drive she would be running all sorts of errands for Dad, like driving to the off licence to pick up his cigarettes after the shops had shut because he was watching Match of the Day.

Our Mum had a fridge, so fresh food shopping could be done locally every week. She didn't have to go out every day because the butcher and baker delivered their goods to us and collected our orders. Before Tesco or Asda started home delivery ,we had door to door service all the while Mum was at home looking after the kids. The baker was a funny looking man; he looked like he had been carved out of driftwood, at least it seemed like it to us. He appeared at the back door regularly three times a week, dressed in a sort of brown overall type of coat which made him look like our school caretaker. He would carry over his arm a large flat basket containing a selection of crusty loaves and rolls which smelt divine and, in the hope of tempting us, cream cakes and doughnuts which we hadn't realised we needed until then. He was a cheery soul, always had a bit of banter with us and we were under the impression that we were one of his favourite families. Indeed, he would often give us some free rolls as we were such good customers.

The butcher would take an order early in the week and deliver the meat in time for the weekend, when of course all mums would be cooking a Sunday roast. We even had a fishmonger at one point, but we didn't like the smell when he opened the back doors of his delivery van. One thing that has stayed the same is the milkman who delivered every day to everyone. You heard him clanking up the road at the crack of dawn in his electric milk float and the comfortingly familiar sound of the empties being collected up would drift in through the window as you dozed in bed. The shop where Mum bought most of the groceries wasn't within walking distance, so it worked like this: she wrote her order for the week in a little red notebook, the grocer took the list when he delivered what she'd ordered the previous week and swapped the notebook with last week's order for the one she'd just written her next order in. The list, if I remember correctly, always included the boring stuff like lard, margarine, butter, bacon, flour, sugar and so on. Luckily there was a greengrocers shop within walking distance and next door to it was a post-office-cum-general-store sort of place where they stocked a vast array of sweets as well as dull stuff like hair grips and greetings cards. This was where we often went to spend our pocket money, if we'd got any. Mum usually gave us two shillings (10p) each pocket money which always went on sweets: sherbet pips, aniseed twist, blackjacks, sherbet dips, spangles, gobstoppers to name just a few of our favourites. Supermarkets were just about to be invented and the concept of self-service was in its infancy. We can remember thinking that this weird way of shopping that had been imported from America would never catch on…

Sometimes on a Saturday, Mum would go off on the bus to do some shopping in town even after we got a car, because for Dad Saturday afternoon was dedicated to watching sport. Football in

Inspiration and Elbow Grease

the cooler months and cricket in the summer. We used to watch for her coming home, excitedly wondering what she might have brought back, because she always did have something for us, even if she'd only gone shopping for clothes. As soon as she came in sight we'd all three rush out to meet her. Occasionally, she might take us shopping in town with her, maybe to buy school uniform or something else equally uninteresting. But we knew she would probably buy us lunch at our favourite fish and chip café. This happened infrequently enough to make it a special treat and therefore a happy memory. Fish, chips, peas and bread and butter washed down with tea in white china cups...

When we were young – very young – housewives, I think I was more intimidated by the butcher's shop than Saggy was. In the 70s we had two butchers within a five minute walk from home. The floors in both these shops were strewn with sawdust to mop up the spilt blood, and nobody thought it gruesome. In one of these shops the butcher used to run his fingers through his hair before handling the meat and even an inexperienced housewife knew that was a bad sign. In the other shop the elderly butcher addressed me as 'madam', which really made me feel like a fraud. In neither shop did I have a clue about the different cuts of meat or what I should do with them. I thought I ought to know about these things and it never crossed my mind to ask the butcher's advice.

When Saggy was in a butcher's shop as a young housewife she heard a customer ask the butcher some technical questions about making gravy from a roasting joint. He pointed at Saggy with his sharp knife and said, 'Ask her'. So Saggy replied, 'Why me?' and he said, *'Because you look like the sort of person that knows how to make gravy.'*

She did, as it happens, but she was not sure if it was a compliment.

In later years one of the smartest things we did was to train up the older kids to help with the weekly supermarket shop. In the days when we used to need two, or even three, trolleys this was a necessity anyway. Children, when they get to a certain age [probably younger than you think], can be brilliant at remembering what you normally buy, checking dates for freshness and basic shopping trolley driving. You can even give them a separate list to go off and do half the shopping themselves and re-join you at the till when they're done. This basic training in checking dates, working out if a deal is really such a deal, budgeting and avoiding impulse buying stands them in good stead for adult life and saves you time and money. It also gives children a sense of pride in their capabilities and the lovely feeling of being needed and part of a team.

Eating Out

We avoided this when possible. Eating out in restaurants and cafes was not something that happened often, if at all, for reasons of expense and logistics. A quick cup of tea in the British Home Stores café where you could just about squeeze a pushchair in was about as good as it got. Everywhere seems so much more family friendly these days.

So, taking a picnic out somewhere was a much better plan. Homemade sandwiches and cake, fruit and possibly crisps were packed in enormous bags and off we all went to the beach or the hills or wherever. Happy days.

Eating Together

We always ate our meals together at the table, at least while the kids were young. This, we felt, would be a time of family togetherness; a time to talk and laugh and share. As it turned out, and perhaps surprisingly, it mostly was.

Inspiration and Elbow Grease

In those early days, the troops were summoned to the table by the ringing of a ship's bell which hung handily on a nearby bracket [Moo] or a brass bell on a bamboo frame from Hong Kong [Saggy]. Dinners were dished up at the table out of huge pots and pans. [We hadn't yet learned the art of presentation]. This was probably a mistake as it gave everyone a good view of the exact amount of leftovers they would be competing for.

The next mistake was to allow the kids to have second helpings as soon as they'd finished the first plateful. This resulted in them racing to finish in order to have the first go at seconds. If they didn't finish quickly enough there wouldn't be any left. With hindsight, maybe I shouldn't have given them another plateful, or at least made them wait until everyone had finished. However, nobody was allowed to eat until everyone had been served. Then the meal would begin as though a whistle had been blown.

Tea times usually involved bread and spreads, cold meat, cheese and occasionally cake. The main rule at this meal, after the imaginary starting pistol had gone off, was 'SOS – Stretch or Starve.' Or help yourselves. Sounds a bit wild, doesn't it? But it wasn't. We did teach them manners too.

Things Get More Complicated

Is there anything so *time consuming* as putting a cooked meal on the table seven days a week for a family? Is there anything so *complicated* as putting a healthy meal on the table for your family seven days a week? Why should it be complicated? Why should it be time consuming?

When we were young mums with lots of kids at home we had two problems concerning food. Well, two problems concerning main meals. The problem was that we wanted to cook from scratch because it's healthier. It is also cheaper to buy the ingredients and cook a meal than it is to buy sauces, ready meals, microwave meals, frozen dinners, takeaways, etc. as well as being better for you. And it's the 'better for you' part of the problem that makes it complicated.

I think our children ate differently from most of their friends when they were small. One of our sons brought a friend home for dinner when he was in primary school. Because I always cooked from scratch, I usually had a pot of stock made from real bones on the Aga, and a range of fresh vegetables in the fridge, together with left over meat from whatever meal we had had the day before. On this particular day I had decided to make chicken stew. We had had roast chicken the day before and I had spent some time pulling the remains of the meat off to keep in the fridge, popping the carcass in a big saucepan with an onion, a carrot and hot water and simmering it half the day. I then took the bones out, threw them away and added pearl barley, chopped carrots, chopped onions, chopped potato and chopped celery. I would simmer it for a bit, and then add some homemade dumplings made with suet.

On the day my son's friend came home, I was a bit apprehensive of serving him the steaming homemade chicken stew with dumplings. Every time my son had been to his house he had been given frozen oven chips with chicken nuggets, or frozen oven chips with pizza or frozen oven chips with fish fingers. Knowing this was the kind of food his little friend was used to, I did wonder how he would react to chicken stew with real vegetables. Whatever he thought at the time, my son later told me that his friend enjoyed it. This could be true, or he could just be very diplomatic.

Not everyone was so diplomatic about our cheap and healthy food. I was away in London one week and I had trained our older children to make dinners. I was quite confident the menus I'd left behind would be made efficiently, deliciously and accu-

Inspiration and Elbow Grease

rately. One of the meals I'd ask the kids to make was tortillas with refried beans. Our family never bought tins of beans already refried that you just had to open, tip into a pan and warm up. No, we would buy tins of kidney beans that we would add to fried onions and garlic with lots of butter and olive oil, turmeric, cumin and other spices including chilli. When hot enough the kidney beans were mashed into the oil, onions and garlic with a potato masher and placed in a hot dish to go in the centre of the table to be spread on the tortillas with salad leaves, sliced onion, grated cheese and cream.

This was in fact a delicious meal. However, when I was in London my children had a foreigner staying who was quite outspoken. My daughter had made the refried beans according to instructions and was bringing the bowl of steamy mashed beans into the dining room to lay on the table. This was not remarkable, it had happened many times before and all my other children had eaten this meal and enjoyed it. Unfortunately, it seemed that this foreign visitor had never seen anything like it before in her life. Instead of just quietly trying it out to see if she liked it, instead of just asking if she could only have a small amount, instead of politely saying 'I'd rather not have some thank you', this girl said something quite rude in a very loud voice along the lines of, 'What the *heck* is that? It looks disgusting! I'm not eating it!'

Getting the Kids Involved

I thought asking the children what meals they want to cook might help them get interested in preparing food rather than them just expecting to sit down to a meal cooked for them every day of the week. This sounds a good idea, and it *is* – though I feel I left it too late for my younger kids. Some of my older children could be given an ox heart and they could slice it up, fry slivers in garlic and herbs while roasting potatoes and preparing a salad. Ox heart is a nutritious and cheap beef meal because, although it is technically classed as offal, it is a muscle meat not a gland which is why people often find liver and kidneys so difficult to swallow.

Three of my kids could turn out a bread dough with fairly minimal effort and good bread it was too. I had some of them bake cakes, make our own ice cream topping, and roast meat. I tried buying some of them their very own cookery books and saying they could choose a day of the week to make a meal and I would buy the ingredients, but it never really took off...

On one memorable occasion I told the kids they could choose whatever they wanted to eat for Christmas dinner. They could vote for their favourite meal whatever it was and we would have it. They chose sausages and chips.

Sausages and chips!

This may have been because everything was usually homemade and healthy at that stage in their lives: shepherd's pie, Alsatian onion tart, paella, stew, lentil rissoles...

Fortunately, after the initial thrill wore off they decided to never do that again, as there was no magic to the meal. The choice had been made to allow more time to open presents as oven chips don't take any prep and not much of a clear up.

Clearing Up: a Competition and a Phone Call

Talking about clearing up after meals, we developed a strategy for clearing up that worked magnificently for many months if not years. It was called by Saggy's family the Five Minute Clear Up and by Moo's family the Mass Clear Up. We had about the same number of kids at the time, and we ate our evening meal at about the same time as each other. At the end of the meal, timers would be set and the signal Go! was shouted. Then we had to get

Inspiration and Elbow Grease

the table cleared, the dishwasher loaded, the hand washing done, the table wiped and the floor swept for the timer to be stopped and a phone call would be made to compare times. The winners took the shortest time.

This developed into a bit of an art so that at the end of the meal we would start stacking the plates at the end of the tables ready to go. We would have made sure the sink was empty ready for the pots and pans. We even started devising meals where there was minimal prep so less clearing up. The lesson learned from this was mainly that, if everybody concentrated and worked quickly together, then the whole meal clear up could be finished in 5 minutes. Part of the reason this started I suppose is that in both families there were individuals who could make clearing up after a meal last all evening.

Chapter 4
Making a Garden

Gardening is cheaper than therapy and you get tomatoes.

Inspiration and Elbow Grease

A Necessity...

If you have kids then a garden is a massive plus. When we had children we always managed to have a garden big enough for them to make dens in, dig to Australia, keep chickens, have a sand pit, learn to swim in a massive paddling pool, grow vegetables, climb trees and generally get very tired and dirty. Our children spent a lot of their childhood dirty; as long as they were happily occupied it was fine by us. In fact, when our two families actually lived next door to each other we ripped the fence out between the two gardens to make one big one. The advantage was that, apart from having more space, the kids had more people to play with. It is easy for your children to get bored with their siblings, but add in a few cousins and the game is on…

We did have some friends with children the same age who came to stay with us one year. The Mum was a very well organised woman who gave her children clean clothes every day and ironed their socks. One day our two sons had spent the morning playing in the garden, and when they came in for lunch their different approaches to play could be clearly seen. My boy was [as usual] filthy. Our friend's son was as immaculate as when he had first put on his freshly laundered T shirt and shorts that morning.

'Have you had a nice morning playing together?' I said naively, ruffling my son's hair.

'Playing?' snorted my son in disgust. 'You can't call what John* has been doing *playing.*'

*Not his real name.

Saggy & Moo

Our kids had a very adventurous approach to their time spent outside. When we have contained them in any of the gardens that we have had, their amusements have always included either, digging very large pits and tunnels or, some species of construction project. I once came out into the garden to see why the children had been unusually quiet for some time to find that they had sorted through a pile of discarded building materials left over from a house project and had constructed a sort of fountain attached to the boundary wall at the end of our property. It included a little pool. Our eldest son was standing there in a mini boiler suit looking very pleased with himself.

Of course there were accidents, so many minor ones to be honest that we got somewhat blasé. One of our daughters had a nasty tumble once that meant she had to have stitches. We had taken her to A&E and at the triage station the nurse had asked calmly how she had come by her injury. She eyed us with suspicion because we had been in a couple of times before when she had been there. I am not sure if she remembered us but she made us feel guilty. When we told her that our daughter had fallen off the washing line she actually stopped what she was doing and said something under her breath which I couldn't quite catch. Then she asked what my husband's job was. When we said 'Health and Safety Consultant' she actually laughed…

One Mum who lived near us had six kids and no real garden. They made use of their paved small yard with such things as skipping and hopscotch but there was no space for letting off steam. This valiant woman used to take her whole family off to the park every afternoon in the school holidays as she knew how important it was for them to run about in the fresh air. She had no car, so she used to walk the half hour it took to reach the swings and grass, spend a couple of hours there, then walk the half hour home. The dedication of this woman put me to shame as all I had to do was open the back door, let them all out and put jugs of water and a bowl of apples on a tray and not see them for ages.

Growing Stuff

We wondered why we both have the urge to get out in the garden at the first hint of Spring and start planting stuff. It has happened every year, ever since the first time we planted seeds and watched them germinate and grow, all those years ago when we were young mums. The magic has never faded. We think we got our love of gardens from our Mum who would far rather be working outdoors than doing housework. To be fair, she would far rather be doing anything than housework. And who can blame her?

Sweeping the garden path and pruning hedges was her way of lending a hand when we had small children; much more useful, she felt, than changing nappies. And for us, up to our eyebrows in carrot puree and squeaky toys, this was fine. We never got much time to 'garden' with young kids. I remember planting seeds every Spring and wondering why they never grew. I now know it is because they need watering and looking after. I thought I could just walk away after sowing seeds and watch a miracle happen. I saw our Mum develop a flourishing garden and envied her. How come she had such success?

Saggy & Moo

Mum – still helping in the garden at 89

She got her love of gardening from her father, who used to take her along with him to his allotment when she was a child, perched on top of a wheelbarrow of manure covered with a sack. During the war, Grandad grew enough vegetables to feed his large family most of the year, which is just as well because they didn't get much else to eat. Rationing meant that a small amount of food had to go a long way so, even though there may have been a rabbit-breeding operation developing in their back yard to supply extra protein, vegetables were a welcome addition to the daily menu. [It was many years later that our Mum found out where all her pet rabbits went...]. But at the allotment Mum was able to eat tiny carrots [the 'thinnings'] fresh out of the ground and to pinch gooseberries from the neighbour's allotment when her Dad wasn't looking. Her job was to go along the rows pulling out weeds with her small fingers. These things are still some of her happiest memories of childhood.

My first memory was from about the age of 3 or 4, when I was at the bottom of the long garden of our first house. Our father had put up a sort of wooden railing behind which we were to grow vegetables. I distinctly remember scratching in the dirt and sowing seeds in the little area he had given to me as 'my plot'. I was so proud and what I wanted to grow were carrots. All my memories are about the digging and the sowing. I have no recollection of the actual pulling up of carrots, or of eating them, just the getting the seeds going. This goes to show how important just the anticipation and joy of working outside is. So, start 'em young…

Childhood Dreams

As children, both of us had dreams of a country lifestyle. We were intrigued by the smallholding adventure, though it must be said that it was at a distance. I think we liked the idea of clucking chickens and wood burning stoves for heating and cooking but had no idea of the reality of such a lifestyle. I lived my fantasy out by having a few chickens in my end-of-terrace garden and buying a four oven Aga. Moo went one or two better than me by moving to a real cottage-in-the-country with a veg garden, chicken coop, pigsty, barns and a paddock.

'Suddenly having a couple of acres,' she said to me once, 'makes you realise what an awful lot of work a small holding or similar would be. It also makes you laugh cynically at the starry eyed townies on 'Escape to the Country' who are unfazed by five acres and think they might like to keep a few goats and chickens, maybe some sheep and grow all their own veg. They have NO idea. We might have inherited a run-down pigsty and I know you wanted me to keep pigs but we couldn't afford the strong fencing needed and pigs are *very good at escaping.* Luckily I was friendly with a mum from the school who warned me not even to *think* about keeping sheep as they can be more trouble than they're worth. A veg patch was all I could manage, even that was a struggle when you have young kids. I still can't believe some townies think they can take on all that WHEN THEY RETIRE!'

The reason *I* wanted pigs is partly because I like bacon and wanted to have the stuff that doesn't ooze white gunge when fried. I fancied my hand at making my own sausages because I had a sausage-skin-filler attachment to my large Kenwood Major machine. But really it was because I still remembered the romantic notions from Laura Ingalls Wilder and their hogs. Although when we were children, the farm at the bottom of our garden included a few pigs and we used to watch them being fed the pigs swill [left over school dinners from the local primary – now illegal]. The farmer warned us not to get too close or the sows would have our arms off. The sows were huge and they often had little piglets with them, which is what would make them aggressive if you got too near. Come to think of it, they did smell very, very bad. Or that might just have been the leftover school dinners...

Seeds and Cuttings

We were usually 'close to the bone' financially when our kids were small and there was no spare cash to splurge at the garden centre on plants, tools, seeds, plant feed etc. but there IS another way. The frugal gardener is undaunted by lack of money. We knew of one enterprising lady who took scissors with her to the garden centre and surreptitiously helped herself to cuttings of any plant that took her fancy. We wouldn't recommend that of course, but it is tempting.

Instead of stealing, make friends with gardeners. When you visit the gardens of family and friends who have plants you like, heap praise on their arrangements, their pruning skills and the vigorous growth of all their specimens. Most of the time they will

Inspiration and Elbow Grease

start offering you cuttings. That is how I have a large selection of beautiful pelargoniums in my conservatory without spending a penny. If you don't know how to *grow* cuttings, ask green-fingered friends the secrets of their success and if you look intensely interested and impressed they may even offer to do it for you…

The same applies to asking for seeds if anyone has some to spare when their flowers have finished. I have just been given a small envelope of Anemone seeds because I couldn't get hold of any online and I was bemoaning this fact in the hearing of someone who grew some. [I didn't know she grew them – it was serendipity at this point]. Then when you have grown your own you can save seeds for next year.

DIY garden projects

You can even tackle projects like patios very cheaply, if you have some ingenuity.

Our Mum showed us how it was done…

Saggy & Moo

When we were children, we moved to a newly built house, so the garden when we moved in was a blank canvas. There was grass, but Mum thought something a bit more solid outside the French windows would be nice; she wanted somewhere to sit and sip sherry in the warm summer evenings. There weren't the funds to have a patio laid so, thinking outside the box as usual, she wheeled an old pram round to where houses were still being built and begged or stole broken bits of paving slabs then pushed them back home. I don't know how many trips she had to make but it must have been quite a few.

Mum masterminded the project and also did the fetching of the materials. Our father would never have been seen wheeling a pram full of broken slabs around or have had the cheek to ask for them, but she managed to rope him in for the construction part. So, when she had hauled home enough bits of slab, Dad set about making crazy paving, fitting the randomly shaped bits of paving slab together in what he considered to be an artistic pattern.

You don't see crazy paving much these days, and with good reason. It looks messy, can be a tripping hazard and is difficult to sweep. But, because our Mum wasn't squeamish and had no pride, we ended up with a patio to sit on that we wouldn't otherwise have had.

Our most famous garden project was when my husband made a chicken coop to satisfy my longing to have my own egg-producing facility. Plus, I liked to hear the clucking. When we were kids there was a farmer's orchard at the end of our garden which contained sheep and chickens and I felt that when there are clucking hens all seemed right with the world. My husband does things properly; he didn't just knock some pallets together; he constructed a small but sturdy house, with window and doors and enough room to stand up inside. He painted it green and placed it behind his workshop and fenced off an area for the

Inspiration and Elbow Grease

chickens to scratch. We had a friend who used to raise chickens and ducks from fertilised eggs who gave us six chicken eggs to hatch. I don't know what the odds are but five of the chicks turned out to be cockerels. Apart from the fact we would not get as many eggs as anticipated, I can imagine our neighbours' response to five cockerels crowing at daybreak every day. You may well expect something of the sort in the country, but we were living in a Victorian end of terraced house. Granted, we had a big garden – but not that big…

We eventually bought six young hens and they provided us with eggs for some time. I liked letting them out to scratch in the garden but they had a tendency to eat anything I was growing. They died off one by one and I suggested that we kill one to eat. I got somebody else to wring its neck but I hadn't anticipated what was involved in the gutting [the smell!]. Nor had I anticipated how long it would take to strip the feathers off. There were no Youtube videos in those days, I just did everything wrong and swore not to gut a chicken again.

Beneficial Extras

At the bottom of our childhood garden was a hazel nut tree and a damson tree. To us kids, they were just trees that were too small to climb so we ignored them. But to our ever-resourceful mother the damson tree meant one thing and that was jam. We had such fun picking up the ripe fallen fruit from the grass while our Mum stood on a shaky pair of steps and picked all the fruit she could reach. She would boil up the fruit with sugar and spoon it into jars and label them with the date. There was loads of the stuff. There would always be bread and jam in our house.

But this whole thing of actually making your own food from what you could find in your garden lit a spark in us that we haven't forgotten. This is why, when I tried and failed to run an allotment with a toddler and baby in tow, I turned my hand to collecting blackberries when we were out for late summer walks. Why I made rose hip syrup from haws that we collected. Why I took foraging books out from the library and bought 'Food for Free' by Richard Mabey. I even collected stinging nettle tops in the Spring and made nettle soup – which was good.

When we moved into the house where we live now, one of the biggest advantages was the two plum trees behind the garage. I remembered my Mum and the damson jam, so I bought a Weck electric preserving pan and a selection of Weck preserving jars and now have rows of golden yellow plums sitting on shelves in a cupboard. This satisfies the alchemist in me and I have a sense of almost homesteading satisfaction that I have captured some of my garden's fresh bounty to feed my family.

One of us [and it isn't me] has inherited our mother's knack of getting stuff to grow. Her garden is full of tomatoes and salad stuff which is thriving. Mine seems to get eaten by slugs. I did buy some potato sacks and grow some potatoes from cut up old spuds that had begun to sprout. One allotmenteer I know told me he had successfully grown a crop of potatoes from just potato peelings. Now that *is* being frugal.

Is it worth it?

The thing to remember about making a garden is – *don't give up.*

My very first garden was temporary, in a rental property of a two bed semi that was £10 a week [1975 prices]. We were only going to stay in it until my husband finished teacher training college, so I had no big designs of constructing anything of lasting value but I did want to grow radishes and stuff. One of the attractions of the garden was that it backed onto a field which sloped down to the river Medway and had fantastic views. It also contained a pony which belonged to our landlord's wife who lived next door.

Inspiration and Elbow Grease

I almost felt like I was living in the country. I loved hanging freshly washed sheets on the line and watching them flap in the breeze that whisked up from the river. I loved patting the forelock of the friendly pony when he came up to the fence. I loved working in the garden with my husband on warm summer days, when he would fling his jacket over the fence post when he got too hot. Except, the very nice jacket got eaten by the pony when we slipped in for lunch. There were bits of it left, but not enough to reconstruct the garment. Bits of cloth dangled out of the pony's mouth and the landlord's wife was very worried that we might have killed it. I was just as concerned about the jacket as we were very poor.

My first proper garden in the house we first bought was going to be a fantastic-food-production-project; I was raring to go and fired with enthusiasm. I bought seeds like there was no tomorrow and filled up pots and planted out and watered and weeded. Unfortunately, I had mainly chosen to grow cauliflowers. Have you tried to grow cauliflowers? They ended up straggly with no firm head, a dingy yellow, and riddled with caterpillars. I almost gave up the whole idea of growing food entirely. If this has happened to you [particularly with cauliflowers] then I urge you to persevere with something else, something easy and foolproof that will boost your confidence. I still can't grow cauliflowers so if anyone has any tips please let me know…

I did try an allotment, but the children were all small and they didn't appreciate the experiment. The actual site was a twenty minute walk away, and I used to trundle the pram with a baby in it, a toddler sitting on a pram seat, with two or three other kids trailing along carrying spades, forks, buckets and seeds. There was no shed on that allotment so I had to take everything with us on each trip.

My first idea, after clearing all the large weeds off, was to cover a large area with thick black plastic to kill off the tiny weeds. This was a complicated procedure with kids flying off in all directions, the baby crying for a feed and a smidgin of arthritis in my lower back. One of the older kids looked at me at the end of a particularly frustrating session and said calmly, 'What's the point? We can buy vegetables at Asda'. In the end I agreed. I did gain another allotment when we moved to a different town and the kids were older. I had a shed and a greenhouse at that one but the whole experience was spoilt when another allotmenteer treated my flourishing nettle patch with weed killer. I had been growing these to make nettle tea with, and they were hidden behind my shed so as not to offend the other gardeners but when I complained to the officials on site they said, 'Don't complain, love. They probably thought they were doing you a favour.' I was furious and walked away.

It is almost impossible not to succeed with chard, or tomatoes, or potatoes. Moo says 'I have never had a problem growing potatoes.' So, later in life I tried and I sort of succeeded too.

Apart from anything else, making a garden is a vote for the future. It is saying that we are constructing something that we can enjoy for years, and that we can leave for other people to enjoy who come after us.

Someone is sitting in the shade today because someone planted a tree a long time ago

Warren Buffet

Inspiration and Elbow Grease

Saggy Tip: If all is lost, throw Calendula seeds at any dirt patch. Then just sit back and watch…

Chapter 5
Making a Plan

> *Good order is the foundation of all good things*
>
> Edmund Burke [1729–97]

Back of an Envelope

Because I had a lot of children that went to school having to look clean and tidy, having had breakfast, having a packed school bag

Inspiration and Elbow Grease

and homework done, letters signed and two matching shoes on their feet, I often left the house in a hurry. This always meant coming home to a big mess – breakfast remains still on the table, beds unmade, games that some child had hoped to have played in the last ten minutes before the mad dash out left opened and scattered across the playroom floor.

The emotional impact this had on me was depressing. I had to clear this mess up before my food shop/ friends coming over/doctor's appointment/or, more terrifying, the arrival of the health visitor to check on whichever baby I had at that time. I know that this may not happen now, but we used to be looked after well by our local surgery. The problem was, *I didn't know where to start*! There was just so much to do! If I cleaned the kitchen, what if a visitor wanted the toilet and there may be a child's underwear and pyjamas still on the floor and toothpaste around the rim of the sink? If the health visitor wanted to check on a sleeping baby in the Moses basket in our bedroom, had I made the bed and were my husband's socks and yesterday's boxers still on the floor? If I had to go straight out to shop, could I put the shopping away on my return if breakfast bowls and sticky islands of jam were still all over the kitchen table?

Then Moo and I found a book that made a pathway through the mess and gave us a scaffolding to hang our time on. It was called *How Do You Find the Time* by Pat King.

She suggested something that was new to us, was fun, and it worked…

As she said, 'I've discovered that I can make a challenging game out of my work by *planning it backwards*… We can sit down at the kitchen table, pour half a cup of coffee, find an old envelope and a pen [or eyebrow pencil or crayon] and make a game of planning backwards.'

Then she advises us to *set a goal*. In my case it could be the health visitor arriving at 12.00. So I set the goal of order by noon and that is written at the top of my list. Next I have to assign each task with a given amount of time [according to how messy it is] and then give it a time slot. The point of the exercise is that when the time is up I walk out of that room and go to the next item on my list. If my kitchen is the messiest area I would have to start at 11.00 if I needed to finish at 12.00. She then gives an example of her timed list and this would be mine:

12.00 Finish
11.00 Start the kitchen clear up
10.40 Clean the downstairs toilet and upstairs bathroom
10.30 Hoover through the playroom and hall
10.00 Pick up games and clothes and toast crusts from the playroom
9.45 Pick up clothes from my bedroom floor and make the bed
9.20 Change baby's nappy, feed and put down for a sleep
9.15 Come back from the school run

This is a timed list, so it is a challenge. It depends on the baby settling and was much easier to follow in later years when all the children were at school. But this is how I started off and it kept me sane.

I had 20 minutes to clean both toilets, that's all. So I kept a spray at each site so I didn't waste time rummaging in my kitchen cupboard looking for cleaning materials. I just had to swish round the basin, squirt stuff in the toilet, pick up towels and put tooth brushes back in the holders. That's all. No time for a deep clean where I would find myself two hours later with the Weetabix still hardening on the cereal bowls.

This was OK when I needed an emergency strategy for a specific day, but I always aimed to organise a week at a time. I suppose at

Inspiration and Elbow Grease

the back of my mind I kept harking back to the Laura Ingalls Wilder books. Here I used to read about a well-ordered approach to life and housework. I knew it was a life from another time, but surely there were tips I could carry on with. I particularly liked the concept of allocated specific tasks to a specific day. A quote from *Little House in the Big Woods:*

After this was done, Ma began the work that belonged to that day. Each day had its own proper work, Ma used to say:

Wash on Monday

Iron on Tuesday

Mend on Wednesday

Churn on Thursday

Clean on Friday

Bake on Saturday

Rest on Sunday

How cool is this? I wanted to organise my life along these lines, mainly because it would establish a routine where everything would get done. It seemed to me an organised way to keep tabs on all the tasks that needed doing in a home. It promised me the chance to keep one nostril above the water.

The Planner

It's not my fault I'm not a good housewife. Let me rephrase that. I am not by nature a well organised, tidy, efficient household management specialist. It is not in my nature, neither was it in my environment. Our dear mother will not mind me saying this, but she wasn't a well organised, tidy, efficient household management specialist either. The guilty party, if one can label it so, must be our maternal grandmother. The poor woman had been in service and so very likely was sick and tired of housework anyway. Our mother's description of her home life was slap-dash, untidy and not altogether clean. I won't embarrass my mother here by describing the sort of conditions they lived in but it was surprising to me as they weren't on the poverty line. Our grandfather had a thriving coal merchant's business, so you would think, wouldn't you, that there was enough money to buy soap and washing soda. I'm not complaining about my grandmother. I didn't even know her very well and I don't think our mother really did either.

I do remember our father saying that he once helped his future mother-in-law spring clean. He heard her mentioning the fact that she needed to do cleaning and he, in order to get into her good books and show her what a lovely husband he was going to make her daughter, offered to help.

Now our grandmother was a sitter. That means she would sit in an arm chair all day and only get up to make a cup of tea. That is an exaggeration, but still. The day came when our father went, all young fresh and eager, to his in-laws' house to help clean and found that it was he, and he alone, who was getting up and pulling curtains down and washing windows and sweeping floors, while his future mother-in-law sat in her chair with a cup of tea.

Our mother in turn would prefer to be in the garden weeding and planting and looking after her flowers, than she would be indoors dusting and hoovering. She would rather clean blocked and smelly drains than dust picture rails. I was never aware of my mother having any household cleaning or organisational plan whatsoever. We were the sort of family that did what we wanted when we wanted and it suited us as children just fine.

Inspiration and Elbow Grease

Our mother would sing songs to us from the bathroom when we went to bed. She would submerge herself in a nice bubble bath leaving the door wide open singing at the top of her voice. She liked to do fun things, she liked to go to work, she liked being part of a choir but she did not like housework. The fact that the four other people in the house never lifted a finger to help her, or very rarely, must have made housework very difficult.

She was never taught to be a well organised housewife and I think this is an important point. It was very difficult for her to pass on knowledge that she didn't have. And of course in those days in the 1950s and 60s there was no Internet and there were no lifestyle programmes. There were a few women's magazines that might do an occasional article on how to run a house and of course there are books but our mum wasn't a book reader.

Our grandmother and our mum may not have been household role models but when we had kids we had a big advantage. We spent a lot of time with foreigners, specifically Dutch and Norwegians. Have you ever been into a Scandinavian home? We both had Scandinavians living with us for time. I remember one Dutch wife in particular would get her children dressed in the bedroom early in the morning, make the bed, sort out the washing piles on the landing and bring the first washing pile down with her so that, as the children were eating breakfast, the first wash load was already going. I, on the other hand, would bring the children downstairs half-dressed or in their pyjamas, feed them breakfast, leave the breakfast dishes on the table while I herded them back upstairs to dress, finished dressing them and then started to sort out the washing. By the time I brought the first wash load down it was getting on for mid-morning.

Another family we had living with us consisted of a mother, father, toddler girl and a baby boy. The wife had lots of paperwork to do and was applying for mortgages and insurances for a new home while the husband was working. I expected her to help me with the housework and in the general running of the home, so we both had lists to do. What impressed me about this housewife was that she would fit the *type of job* she had to do into the *type of time* she had at her disposal. So that, while the children were awake, she would be doing the washing or clearing up, or cleaning and very often the children would be around her playing. But as soon as those two had their midday nap, the mum would stop all practical tasks even if she was in the middle of them, get out her paperwork, and start concentrating in a way that she couldn't do when those children were awake. In this way she suited the task she had to do to the environment she was in.

It slowly dawned on us that if you had children in the home you couldn't always do what you wanted to do when you want to do it. It also gradually dawned on us that if you lived in a muddle things got lost, jobs didn't get done, and things took longer to do in general.

We *eventually* realised if you have kids you need to plan...

We know we have had more kids than is strictly normal but our most manic times were when we had just the first two, as we had to look after more than one person at a time and it confused us. It soon became clear that, if we were to get through the day/week/month/the rest of our lives sane, then we would have to adopt some mechanism of organisation. Remembering those efficient foreigners, we decided to get our act together. If they could do it, so could we.

Now, people that know us well can testify that 'being organised' isn't our strong suit [glad our husbands aren't likely to read this...] but needs must we always say. And needs there certainly were.

Before we reveal the lengths we were driven to in order to keep one nostril above the water, we will add a disclaimer;

Inspiration and Elbow Grease

Systems have to be followed to have a chance of working and a] we didn't always follow them and, b] depending on our state of health and level of the kids' cooperativeness, they didn't always work when we did try to follow them...

But hey, we all get sick days, and kids on wild sprees, and days when everything goes WRONG, but hand on heart, we can truly say that having some sort of framework is like a comforting scaffolding to hang your life on, and to come back to as if to a raft on a choppy sea. Because that is what systems *are*. They are scaffolding, designed to hold your life together while you are working on it. Systems can be a scary concept, but think of it like this. Our way was to write down what we needed to get done in a week and then allocating time to it, making sure we didn't forget ~~anything~~ the most important stuff, and that was our system. That's all. So, the more kids that came along the more we had to plan and write down and it made us look organised when we weren't really, we were just surviving.

My own first attempts at planning were ripping pages out of note books and making a list of everything I had to do THAT DAY, which was fine as far as it went, but days would suddenly pop up out of nowhere and I would find it was someone's birthday that I had forgotten. I had forgotten because I was concentrating on one day at a time and not looking ahead. At all. Now, there *are* times when we must do this [just given birth, bereavement etc] but, in the main a little bit of looking ahead saves time and upsetting your mother-in-law.

∼

I am now going to reveal to you something I devised together with Moo when we were both eyebrow deep in kids. I truly believe we were the pioneers of all the swanky business/life planners that all these cool entrepreneurs are trying to sell us. I called mine 'Memory'.

It was a scruffy old notebook, but it contained gold dust. So, here's how it worked:

1. Open out a spiral-bound notebook so it lays flat and you have a double page spread looking up at you.
2. Get a ruler and pencil and draw columns. On the first page draw a narrow, medium and wide column.
3. On the second [facing] page draw a narrow, wide and then medium column. Ish.
4. So across the two pages we have six columns of varying widths.
5. Then divide the first five columns into seven rows by drawing six equally spaced horizontal lines leaving the last column to run undivided down the page.
6. First column call DAY, Second column DATES TO REMEMBER, third column JOBS & PLANS, fourth column MENU, fifth column LOCAL SHOPPING and last column SUPERMARKET

The planner worked in this way:

Inspiration and Elbow Grease

- Each week you filled in the day and date in the first column.
- In the second column, Dates to Remember, you would fill in any birthdays, anniversaries, weddings or hospital/GP/optician/school appointments.
- In the third column, you planned your jobs for the week. As you could see which days were heavy with appointments you could devise a work schedule that left that day free.
- In the fourth column, you would plan a menu for the whole week, making sure you kept simple or reheated meals for complicated days.
- In the next column, you would fill in the local shop. In the days of Post Offices this was great as you could make sure you bought the birthday cards and stamps a few days before the birthday came up in the Dates to Remember column. Or you could buy your fresh meat from the local butcher at the beginning of the week because you had looked at your menu.
- The last column was Supermarket [or weekly] shop, which is not divided up horizontally. The idea of this is that if you leave the planner open on the side, as soon as you run low of something you write it down straight away in this column and it is automatically part of your next weekly shop. The rest is added by looking down at your menu for the week.

OK, so we don't all have local shops anymore [this was from 1984 after all], and it may well be too labour intensive for busy working mums to draw up every week. But you must admit, in the early 1980s, we were ahead of the planning game.

Chapter 6
Making an Attempt...
...at raising healthy, kind, hardworking kids.

> *There is scarcely any less bother in the running of a family than in that of an entire state. And domestic business is no less important for being less important.*
>
> Montaigne [*Essais*]

All Work and No Play?

I sometimes wonder what sort of impression I gave my children of being a housewife. Some of the older ones repeatedly insisted that they weren't having any kids. I listened to this for years with the growing sense of failure. But one day I took a deep breath and asked why. The answer came as quick as a swipe from Obi Wan's light sabre: *too much work.*

Work? *Work*? When normality to them was getting up at 11:00 am, and clearing the table was their definition of a daily chore? When merely pairing their socks and putting them in the washing basket was a tad too demanding?

What did they know about work?

In the holidays, my teenagers used to live life by one timetable and my husband and I by another. They went to bed about midnight and slept round the clock. My husband and I went to bed earlier, got up earlier and possibly bumped into the teenagers around lunchtime [which they referred to as breakfast]. Have you ever tried cooking a stir fry, soaking egg noodles in hot water, crushing garlic and attempting special fried rice with a group of semi-conscious young adults stumbling around in the kitchen looking for tea bags?

They would file in one by one, dressed in boxers or skimpy nighties. All were barefoot so all would squeal in succession if they stood in the water slopped out of the dog bowl, or squelch in the soggy remains of a used tea bag they had dropped in their stupor. They were lured from their beds by the smell of frying. They assumed I was cooking breakfast.

I would try to push them out of the kitchen saying, 'No this is *lunch*', but the thought would fail to connect. So I would press a mug of tea into their hands with the information that we would be eating in only 15 minutes.

Inspiration and Elbow Grease

They could never wait 15 minutes.

They were starving, they were growing teenagers. So they would grab biscuits, sandwiches made on the hoof and a handful of satsumas before stumbling back to their own rooms. I would then have a second breakfast preparation to clear up while getting a midday meal that half the family would be too full to eat.

And what about the jobs I had planned? Holidays could be a great time for harnessing the working potential of your kids, right? I would have hopes of one mowing the lawn, one baking a cake, one ironing, one clearing up the front room after yesterday's late night supper. But when I realised the queue that had formed for the shower I just wondered if they would be dressed by teatime.

After a week or two of this I would rebel, like a frustrated teenager with parents who cramp her style. I would make a curfew. Breakfast *absolutely* over by 10:00 am, and no food *whatever* till lunch. Period, as the Americans say.

I rode the tidal wave of mutinous cries with the grim determination shown by Montgomery at El Alamein. Heroically, I banged on all bedroom doors and pulled quilts off at 9:30 am shouting, 'No breakfast if you're not downstairs in 30 minutes!' I was on a mission. As the 15th century proverb says, *the day is short and the work is long.*

There would be moans, 'What are you *like* mum', and 'I don't *believe* this!'

But hey. They did begin to stumble down about tenish for the rest of the holidays and some of them were even dressed. They didn't fancy the responsibilities and chores related to parenthood then, but I hope their future employers were thankful.

Holidays! I sort of liked them because there are none of those hellish deadlines. And yet...

I know that teenagers live under a lot of academic pressure, peer pressure and life is stressy. I know we need to be supportive, understanding and flexible. But if a lad never understands the sheer practicality of pairing dirty socks, it's a poor show. If a young girl can't cook a single meal before she leaves home she will probably regret it. I know I did.

To be fair, youth is a time of extremes. Ecstatic highs followed by depressing lows. Bursts of enthusiasm followed by lengthy boredom. I came home once to discover they had cleaned up the kitchen. They sometimes would suddenly spring clean their bedrooms or radically overhaul the garden. One of them got out the Brasso and shone all the copper water pipes in the utility room. I never found out why.

Teenagers are a whole new ball game. Once you could control what your children wore, what they ate, where they went and what time they went to bed. Not anymore. The discomfort of imposing any timetable on a group of rebels can be scary at first, but it's necessary if we're going to raise responsible adults at the end of it all.

What can we expect then as mothers?

I say, expect nothing and you won't be disappointed. But have a long term hope and you might be pleasantly surprised.

Maybe, just maybe we can follow Theodore Roosevelt's advice;

'Teach boys and girls alike that they are not to look forward to lives spent in avoiding difficulties; teach them that work, for themselves and also for others, is not a curse but a blessing; seek to make them happy, to make them enjoy life, but seek also to make them face life with steadfast resolution...'

Inspiration and Elbow Grease

Taking a Break...

Kids have to go to school or you will be fined. In the old days we could keep them off if they felt tired and nobody minded much. We didn't do it often but it sure did ease off the pressure.

When we had five children in Junior School, we felt that they deserved some sort of mini break. I can't remember exactly why we planned it, but the time came when I felt that we all needed a holiday in term time and August was too expensive as all the prices went up. We came across this lovely apartment for rent in a local Exmoor village. It was above a fish and chip shop which was convenient and it was in a lovely old building. The access to the apartment up on the first floor was through a stone-flagged communal hallway with a Turkish rug on the floor and antique furniture lining the walls. There was a little door in the wall with a latch that looked like a cupboard but when you opened it there were winding stairs up the apartment.

The apartment was quite spacious with two bedrooms, a bathroom and a rather lovely open plan living/dining/kitchen area. It was kitted out in a New York apartment style with large windows opening out onto the street below. We booked a long weekend – go Friday come back Monday. A slight problem was the children were due to be in school Friday and Monday.

Friday morning when the children woke up it was the usual, *I don't want to get out of bed* attitude and to be fair the children seemed extremely tired. I called them into our bedroom and set them on the bed where they looked droopy and almost ill. So I said to them, how about you don't go to school today? I said how about we go on holiday?

The almost instant change in their demeanour was nothing short of miraculous. Gone were the tired and haggard expressions. Gone were the drooping shoulders.

Eyes bright and suddenly very, very alert, they all maintained they suddenly felt fine to a man. They left the room in a cloud of dust and began to pack.

Those few days were what I call 'restorative medicine' and the children benefitted from walks on the moors, open fires, painting, reading and a library visit. We didn't spend much money and we didn't need to. I don't remember any school official complaining that we took our kids out of school without permission. But please don't do that now or you could be in very, very deep trouble. The state cares. My point is that I felt the kids needed a spontaneous break and for many weeks after that there was less trouble getting them off to school.

The Problem of School

Usually school mornings were a battlefield, and however much I tried to plan the night before there was always some sort of last-minute problem on the day. And it was always a different problem.

I would pair shoes and leave them in a row in the hallway because some of the kids would have a habit of losing one of the pair. But in the morning, even though the shoes were fine, someone had mislaid their reading record. If I checked the reading record *and* the shoes, someone else would have forgotten they had swimming that day. I eventually realised that I could not live by my wits when I had kids at school. I could not think on the hoof, I could not muddle through and keep sane.

This is one of the occasions when I was forced into planning to stop my life falling apart and to keep my marbles. There are oh so many planners out there today but I just used paper, a pencil and inspiration. I suppose I constructed spreadsheets before I knew what they were. Similar in effect to the general planner [Chapter 11] which Moo and I put together out of desperation,

Inspiration and Elbow Grease

my school day planner was a substantial checklist of who went to what school, uniform requirement, PE days, book days and what was needed each day of the week for each child.

Unfortunately, one piece of information I always missed putting on the spreadsheet was *who their form tutors were and what class they were in.* If ever I phoned the school about a child and they asked what class my kid was in I had no idea. If they asked me who their form tutor was I would start describing what they looked like. Sometimes I even got that wrong and was a couple of years out of date.

But this I did manage:

1. I planned the breakfast the day before,
2. I laid out school uniform,
3. I doubled checked for book days,
4. I tripled checked for letters in school bags, for trips, for consent forms.

My own kids now have kids of their own and all sorts of information is sent to them via their school's website. Reminders about trips, consent forms and book days are all there at the touch of a button. I had to rely on my kids sharing info with me when they got home. Exactly.

But I had an advantage that very few mums have today. I didn't go out to work. I had time in the morning to make my kids pancakes stuffed with banana and maple syrup. Or do some scrambled egg on their [homemade] toast. And I used to make the kids help.

When I was a teenager, in one of the Laura Ingalls Wilder books I had been struck by the fact that the kids were expected to clear up after their own meals and help their mother tidy up in general:

Laura and Mary helped Ma with the work. Every morning there were the dishes to wipe. Mary wiped more of them than Laura because she was bigger, but Laura always wiped carefully her own little cup and plate. By the time the dishes were all wiped and set away, the trundle bed was aired. Then, standing one on each side, Laura and Mary straightened the covers, tucked them in well at the foot and the sides, plumped up the pillows, and put them in place. Then Ma pushed the trundle bed into its place under the big bed.

[*Little House in the Big Woods*]

And so, right from the age of four and a half, my eldest child would be balancing on a stool washing up the plastic mugs and plates her younger siblings had used for breakfast while I fed the baby, before setting out taking her to reception class at the local infant school.

Bedtime & Homework

Bedtime is inevitable and has to be got through somehow. Having a routine will keep you sane, you may veer off the routine when necessary, but having a scaffolding to hold on to is a lifesaver. Plus, kids will know where they are and will benefit from a regular bedtime. Sounds boring, maybe is boring, but it is the bedrock of a well-ordered family. This takes time to get right. I always seemed to struggle at this but I kept trying. Because, if you had ever come to our house when the kids were young, I wouldn't have advised that you should come at bedtime. Then, any reputation that I did have as a well organised, placid mother, would totter on the brink of total and absolute collapse.

I always tried to develop a fool-proof routine for getting my children into bed at a reasonable time every night. The fiasco would begin straight after tea. Surveying a table full of faces they would look positively cherubic, but I was not deceived. My orders

Inspiration and Elbow Grease

started off being issued clearly and slowly so that everyone would know what they had been asked to do. There would be a general hustle and bustle, a pushing and shoving, then suddenly the kitchen was nearly empty.

I would have a baby waiting for a feed as I wiped peanut butter off the toddler's face, off his hands and hands, off the walls, the highchair and the floor, and start off upstairs. The daily bed race would be on and, as always, I would be determined to get it right.

One such evening went like this:

I dispatched the two eldest girls to the bathroom with firm instructions not to play. Giving the baby to the eldest boy to cuddle, while I began to undress the pre-schooler. Disentangling the toddler from her nappy, I would discerned squeals of high glee coming from the bathroom. This was not consistent with merely washing. The toddler wandered off naked as I ventured along the passageway to investigate: who showed my kids how to flick sodden balls of toilet paper up at the ceiling so that they stick there? Reminding them of what they were supposed to be doing, I suddenly remembered a little nappy-less girl in the front bedroom. But I was too late, she had already performed on the carpet.

The girls emerged from the bathroom in their underwear and go in search of night clothes. I scurried the two youngest into the bathroom for a quick splash during which one of them dropped the clean and dry towels in the water and then broke the soap into little tiny fragments while his sister rummaged around in the bin for Daddy's used razor blades.

Gathering them together I re-entered the bedroom where innocent amusement was occasioned by one of the kids putting her legs down the arm holes of her pyjama top and her trousers on her head. Her sister was clucking around the room flapping her elbows in and out like a chicken. I didn't ask why.

The baby was becoming desperate for a feed so putting the toddler in her cot with a toy and giving her something to play with in the hope that she would amuse herself quietly, I heroically decided to read the three eldest a story and feed the baby at the same time. Our stories were always punctuated by, "What does so and so mean?" Or "What? What?" from the boys while the eldest shouted, "Oh shut up you! Go on mummy..."

Having worked my interrupted way through the adventures of a wooden farmer and his wife, I realised one of the kids was missing. The baby was put in her crib, one boy was sent to undress, the girls asked to tidy up and I set off in search of him. I found him in the bathroom. What did he hope to achieve by rubbing in half a bottle of my body lotion into his hair just before bedtime? As I rinsed the worst off I noticed that time was getting on and nobody as yet was actually settled for the night. I decided to become brisk.

Marching back into the bedroom, to my despair I not only found that one of the girls had drawn a moustache and a pair of glasses on the toddler in felt tip, but that the eldest boy was sitting on top of the wardrobe [still fully clothed]. Fighting down a rising feeling of impatience, I asked him what exactly he was doing on top of the wardrobe. He said he was looking for his tractor.

I tucked a still somewhat damp younger boy up in his little bed with orders not to move and helped a sadder but wiser older boy undress and sent him off to the bathroom, where he kept me informed of his progress in a voice calculated to reach me if I was halfway down the street with ear plugs in. I'm glad my neighbours had children too.

Meanwhile, the girls had tidied up what I asked them to, but unfortunately they had also decided to stage a song and dance

Inspiration and Elbow Grease

act for the benefit of the toddler who was highly impressed. Their hopes of a lively evening's entertainment dashed, the younger girl submissively removed her dark glasses and the pants she had pulled on her head by way of a hat, and the elder girl reluctantly took off Daddy's shirt and my shoes which she had quietly filched from our bedroom. Perhaps one might be firmer if one didn't find it so funny, but by this time another half an hour has gone by and the feelings of inadequacy were beginning to sweep over me.

I scurried the children who were still wandering around into bed and switched off the light. Tidying up after they were all in bed, I came across two books, one shoe, an apple core and several sweet wrappers in the toilet. In the bathroom somebody had been trying their hand at modern art with the toothpaste. I wiped it off the sink, the taps and the rim of the bath and, pausing only to scrape the balls of toilet paper off the ceiling, I made my way downstairs at last.

Just as I was beginning something constructive in the front room, a child I had vainly imagined tucked up for the night would be seen sliding down the bannisters. Apparently I forgot to kiss him. The omission having been rectified, he was told to show his face again at his peril. The girls would go through the usual routine of calling, 'I just need to go to the toilet mummy', and 'I'm thirsty can I have a drink', and, 'it's too hot', and 'I'm too frightened to sleep'...

The sixth time a girl came down with complaints that she couldn't get to sleep, I would point out that it is difficult to sleep when one is constantly walking up and down the stairs. I gave her one of my stern looks and she disappeared, quickly realising the game of *how far we can push mummy* is nearing a close.

Visitors were never actively encouraged at that time of day. Although when the GP popped in after I had had one of the children, he of course came at bedtime. The children had been bathed, half of them were in their pyjamas half of them were totally naked. The bathroom was strewn with talcum powder and soaking wet towels. I was pink and hot, my hair falling in damp strands over my forehead and the toddler was pulling up my skirt. The rest of the children milled around excitedly.

He climbed the stairs, surveyed the scene spread before him, smiled and said, 'It's nice to see you're resting.'

Chapter 7
Making Money Go Round

Use it up, wear it out, make it do, or do without.
Boyd K. Packer

Our Financial Background

Maybe we were programmed to be frugal. Our mother never wasted anything if she could help it. She would even pick up bits of string and elastic bands in the street dropped by the postman and bring them triumphantly home to hoard them 'in case they come in handy'. Even now it's very hard to get her to spend money on herself or throw anything away. She wasn't as extreme as *her* mother though who, after washing all the family laundry (including underwear), would use the disgusting scummy water to wash dishes in. "I can't waste all that hot soapy water", she'd say. Let's hope none of us ever need to resort to that.

On the other hand, maybe we were also programmed to be slap-dash with money because Mum was balanced out, financially speaking, by Dad whose approach to managing money was to spend it if the fancy took him. His was the classic 'If it's in the bank I can spend it' approach. He'd forget there were bills to be paid before the next pay day. Mum used to dread him going shopping because he always came back with more than he went out for.

There was the time, for example, when he went out to buy a small transistor radio and came back having bought a massive radiogram. He didn't get this tendency from Grandma Mary, his mother, but thankfully she gave *us* useful tips on how to manage a small income (and make an amazing stew). Everything else about making the money go round we had to find out for ourselves. We had a lot to learn.

Starting Out

We started our families in the 1970s when purse strings were tight. We had the Winter of Discontent, [if you are too young to know what that is, Google it] the Three-Day Week [ditto],

Inspiration and Elbow Grease

frequent power cuts, drought and food shortages in that decade. Not the best time to start a family, you might think, but luckily none of that put us off having children.

There was little in the way of childcare or flexible working available. It would have cost more to go out to work than it did to stay at home. Having no freezer, microwave or – in the early days – no disposable nappies or automatic washing machines meant there was an *awful lot* to do at home anyway. There was very little in the way of convenience foods except for the tinned sort and practically nothing ready-made frozen. Fish fingers were available of course but, if you are limited to the ice box in the fridge for storing frozen stuff, you tend not to buy much anyway.

We had to find ways to make household income go as far as possible.

So let's rewind a bit and remind ourselves what finances were like for a young homemaker in the 1970s.

Wages were often paid weekly in cash. Utility bills came quarterly by snail mail. You could go to the council offices to pay the rates (Council Tax) and to the Post Office to pay utility bills. Or you had to post a cheque when the bill arrived and make sure you had enough in the bank to cover it when it eventually dropped on the mat.

Child benefit was called Family Allowance and was not paid for the first child. You collected Family Allowance from the Post Office and tried to avoid the long queue of pensioners collecting their weekly pension. There would often be unemployed people cashing their dole giro cheques. Post Offices were very busy places in those days.

Supermarkets closed every day at 5.30pm, except for late closing at 7pm once a week. In our town there was half day closing for all shops on a Wednesday. Some shops would also close in town on a Saturday afternoon and *all of them* closed on Sundays. So if you were working, or had no access to a car outside of working hours, you didn't have many opportunities to do a weekly shop.

When it came to applying for a mortgage, you could only borrow up to two and a half times your annual income and we saw interest rates soar to 14 or 15%. A wife's income [if she had one] was not taken into account in case she had a baby in the future and couldn't go out to work.

Quite a different landscape back then, but we think the principles of managing household finances are still pretty much the same.

What Our Grandmother Taught Us

We used to see our Grandma Mary often when we were kids. Sometimes she came to stay and look after us in the school holidays while Mum was at work. We regularly visited her in her home, where we could be sure she would tell us to look in the sideboard. Here we would find a bag of sweets and a comic each. The 'Dandy' for Moo, the 'Beano' for Saggy and the 'Buster' for Squidge. She was living on a tiny widow's pension, but she always managed to have enough money to buy us that treat.

She taught us the basic principles of budgeting. Each week she collected her pension in cash from the Post Office. At home, she would put a small amount by for each of her bills in a purse with lots of sections – so much in this section for the electric bill, so much in that for the rent, so much in another for the gas bill, and so on. When she had put away a week's worth toward the bills, she told us, she knew whatever was left she could spend.

The two big lessons she taught us were:

1. Make sure you can pay your bills

2. Don't buy what you can't afford

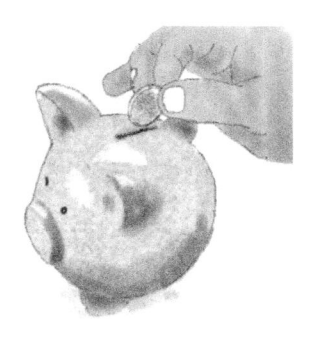

Furnishing a Home on a Budget

We have gleaned so many good things for our homes from second hand shops, reclamation yards and car boot sales. It's much more fun for the frugally minded homemaker to forage this stuff out than to visit stores where it's all done for you and you have to pay through the nose for it. It puts your own individual stamp on your home and makes it yours in a special way.

We had a young friend, a teenage girl, who used to come and give us a hand occasionally when the kids were little. Her special talent was the ability to tidy and arrange things in a room so cleverly that it looked amazing, without adding anything at all. This is a great gift if you can't buy new stuff. You just arrange what you DO have in a different way.

Every so often we would start to look thoughtful, stare speculatively at the furniture in one of the rooms, then come out with a phrase our husbands dreaded.

"I've been thinking..."

What we'd been thinking usually involved heavy lifting [not our department] because it's amazing what a difference just rearranging the furniture can make without spending anything at all.

Sometimes we had to make do with less than ideal furniture until we could afford better. At one time our stop gap solutions in the dining room were as follows:

There was a period of time when the whole family wouldn't have fitted round a normal table and we couldn't afford the huge kind that would have been more suitable. So we made do with an improvised table. When I say table what I mean is a huge board on top of an old dining table. All topped off with a heavy-duty PVC tablecloth. It didn't look too bad, it was the assortment of chairs that let the whole ensemble down.

We temporarily had to use a combination of plastic garden chairs and an old church pew for seating. The pew looked pleasantly quirky and had the advantage of sturdy safety. The garden chairs on the other hand looked rather strange and were definitely not safe. Some of the kids had a habit of 'riling' on their chairs. Riling was a term I believe our Mum invented and it meant tipping the chair back and balancing on the back legs. If you do this on a plastic garden chair the legs buckle, and you end up on the floor. Quite often at mealtimes one or other of the kids would suddenly disappear for a few moments before rejoining us trying to look as if nothing had happened. It wasn't too long before the garden chairs were replaced with something a lot sturdier.

Auctions

You can pick up some brilliant furniture at auctions for very little money, and we did. With a bit of up-cycling, you can turn things into beautiful, useful and bespoke items for your home. Once we bought a large range of solid wooden cupboards for £10 at auction and these were turned into very attractive kitchen cupboards for next to nothing.

As sisters we both loved auctions but we only went to an auction together once. There was this large rug, more of a carpet really, which we both liked the look of. So intent were we on bagging that rug that we didn't notice that we were the only people bidding and we were therefore bidding against each other.

Anyway, one of us got it in the end at about three times the price she could have paid.

How We Afforded Christmas

One question we were asked more often than any other by strangers was 'How do you manage at Christmas?' I can see where they were coming from with this. It must have seemed to most people like a financial and logistical nightmare for a big family.

But we always managed to make a good time for the children. Yes, it was hard work, but we had some lovely times at Christmas. Things weren't too complicated, there wasn't enough money to go mad. It never occurred to us to get into debt to buy the kids fancy presents, but they didn't mind [at least they tell us they didn't]. We weren't pressured by ads on TV because we didn't have one. We made our own family traditions, kept things reasonably simple and enjoyed ourselves.

As with everything else, it took planning and lots of thinking ahead. We also pinched ideas from other people, which is something we have always been good at anyway.

Our strategy for Christmas included:

- Starting early
- Buying second-hand
- Making our own cards and wrapping paper
- Making notes when we had ideas for presents

You can't afford to leave things to the last minute if you have a large family. We found it a good idea to keep our eyes peeled throughout the year for ideas for presents and if we spotted something to either buy it or make a note of the idea. Of course, we were quite happy to buy preloved items if new ones were out of our price range. The children would rather have had these than gone without something they really wanted.

How much nicer to give cards that you have made yourself. Kids enjoy making stuff, so getting them involved with card making is a double benefit. This applies to making your own wrapping paper too. We would buy an industrial roll of heavy brown Kraft paper and then use stamps to apply little prints all over. Home-made presents were something we resorted to at times for the wider family and friends, such a great idea when you want to give but have to stretch the budget. We have given home-made chutney, cookies, spiced nuts and even calendars in the past.

I had to find a way to save my sanity on Christmas mornings because it seemed that the kids were waking earlier every year.

When it got to the stage that the eldest daughter woke up half an hour after midnight all excited and ready to start the day, I knew something had to be done. I made all the children a small Christmas stocking with their own name tape stitched inside. These were brought out every year on Christmas Eve. I would leave them by their beds after they had fallen asleep, ready for them to find on Christmas morning. Inside each would be a satsuma, some nuts or sweets, a little bag of chocolate coins, a few small gifts and something to occupy them [like a comic] so that they didn't wake us up before a reasonable hour.

Mending

Making do and mending featured largely in our lives. It was still normal to make some of your own and your family's clothes and mend them when they wore out instead of throwing them away. We even used to mend tights, either with stitches or a dab of clear nail varnish to stop them laddering.

There was always a mending basket/pile on the go. Rarely did we ever manage to empty it. Mostly it was patching the knees of trousers, mending ripped seams and tears and repairing hems that had come adrift.

Occasionally, we tackled the more advanced stuff, like turning collars, darning socks and – venturing beyond clothing – turning sheets 'sides to middles'. This was when unfitted sheets had worn so thin in the middle you could just about see through them. You'd cut the sheet down the middle and sew the two edge lengths together. This would result in a seam down the middle of your sheet but saved you from having to buy a new one.

Eventually, after making clothes, sheets and towels last as long as possible, things would wear out or become too scruffy to wear any more even for playing in the dirt. Instead of just throwing them away we would try to squeeze the last drop of use out of them. Clothing could be cut up and used as rags. Every self-respecting homemaker had a ragbag. Sometimes we would use the fabric to make something else. For example, when my eldest girl was a toddler, I made a dress for her out of the dress I was wearing when I met my husband.

Towels, if there wasn't a dog in the family to pass them on to, were cut up and hemmed or edged with blanket stitch and transformed into cleaning cloths.

Clothes

We made some of the children's clothes ourselves but mostly we relied on hand-me-downs especially in the early days. We did our best to keep the family in jumpers and cardigans by knitting whenever we had the time.

Clothes weren't as cheap when we were young parents, which is why we had to look after them and make them last as long as possible. Then, once they were outgrown, they would be handed down to the next child. If there wasn't a younger child available in our own family, the clothes might be offered to another family. If nobody else had immediate use for them, the clothes would be stored in the loft until, at last, somebody grew into them. In those days our loft spaces looked like a well organised jumble sale. We were great fans of jumble sales and became experts on which ones were likely to yield a good haul. Mostly these would have been in well to do areas. Coming home with full black sacks from a jumble sale caused great excitement in those days.

When we were teenagers, our dad ran a local youth football team and he volunteered to store the jumble which was being collected for their fundraising sales in our garage. So our jumble training began very early. It was great fun to be the first ones to get a look at the bargains, although we weren't allowed anything free. In later years, when attending other people's jumble sales, we'd have to make sure we were near the front of the queue when the doors opened as there was always an almighty surge for the best stuff when they did.

We found some really nice clothes at jumble sales, for the children and for ourselves. When we needed wool for knitting, we would find old jumpers in colours we liked, unpick them, wash the yarn and roll it into balls then knit them up into new clothes or colourful blankets to add to the cosy feeling of the home. We have never turned our noses up at charity shop clothes. Some of our best bargains came from them. You just never know what you might find.

What we Learned about Budgeting

At times, over the many years we have been homemaking and bringing up our children, we have experienced hardship. At times we have had to scrimp to feed and clothe our families. Now we are older we can look back and assess what was worth doing and what didn't work so well.

In a nutshell, here are the basic principles that we have hewn with our little hatchets out of an immense mountain of wisdom...

Saggy & Moo

1. Don't buy what you can't afford
2. Give children experiences rather than expensive things
3. Keep tabs on spending
4. Planning ahead saves money and time
5. Sort out your priorities
6. Teach children how to manage money
7. Have the mindset to see frugality as a challenge to test your metal. You can do this

---

Think of frugality as a game. Maintaining a frugal lifestyle will be difficult if you're stuck in the mindset that saving money is something you must do because you're poor. If you consider thriftiness a game... the task will be much more enjoyable.

Amy Hoover

Chapter 8
Making Memories

I crown thee king of intimate delights, fire-side enjoyments, home-born happiness.
William Cowper [1791-1800]

Saggy aged 3 [L] Moo aged 5 [R]

We had a lot of fun when we had children at home, whether finances were tight or not. For us it was a major feature of home-making and child rearing. Maybe an extension of the sense of fun we experienced as children. Possibly we just thought it was normal to get fun out of the everyday. Many years after we had grown up a neighbour from our childhood days said how he envied us because he could so often hear laughter coming from our home.

When it came to making our own fun without spending anything, we had a good role model in our dad. With his brother, he invented indoor golf which was played with a ping-pong ball and a back scratcher. It kept them amused for hours but we didn't get much of a look in. They also used to have a reel-to-reel tape recorder and wrote and recorded their own plays and other bits of nonsense, then made us listen to it.

Grave Spotting

For us there was shove ha'penny on the dining room table, board games, card games played for matchsticks, Grave-Spotting and Uncle Hunting. Grave Spotting needs a special mention as we played this a lot. The hours of fun us kids had Grave Spotting shouldn't be underestimated. We had to choose old, spooky Victorian graveyards and the two adults and five children would be divided into two teams. One or two people would go off and scour the graveyard for interesting names. The rest would then be let loose to hunt for them. This is not as easy as it sounds. Then we would choose new 'spotters' at the next graveyard. One object of the game was to find the most bizarre name on a gravestone, the other was to see who could spot it first. We made lists of the names on gravestones which amused us. This sounds more morbid than it actually was. We still remember our favourite name which Saggy found when she was about 10. It was:

Benjamin Bumstead Rackstraw

If anyone has this individual in their family tree, please let us know.

Inspiration and Elbow Grease

Let's talk of graves, of worms, and epitaphs...
Richard lll Act 3

Uncle Hunting

The Uncle Hunting game was a thrill because it was played at the dead of night and only really open to people who had an uncle, specifically a Mad Uncle who didn't mind being hunted. Our Dad used to take us three kids with his brother [the uncle who was going to be hunted] and Uncle's two sons. Uncle would be sent off into the valley which bordered our home. He would have a torch because it was dark, but no mobile because this was the 1960s so if he got very lost he would be in deep trouble. We would choose a night with no moon just to make it more difficult and hope his torch battery ran out.

After Mad Uncle had been released into the wild we would break off into two teams and, after a decent interval, go off in pursuit. A bit like fox hunting without the foxes. Or the dogs. Or the horses. The first group to find Mad Uncle would win. The best part was that we all got wet, muddy and hungry. We would burst home in a rush for hot water and food to be met by our mother who, looking at our sodden frames, would calmly say, 'Did you get your feet wet?'

Miscellaneous

We had the kind of mum who let us make extensive dens in the living room, slide down the stairs on mattresses, make cardboard box houses for Sindy dolls all over the living room, go out scrumping in the Kent orchards, paddle unsupervised in the village stream, climb trees and make dens in the orchard across the road. [Actually, we're not sure she knew about the mattresses. Or the scrumping.].

We must have been *very happy* at school, because our favourite game during the summer holidays was playing being at school. Before you dismiss us as really pathetic kids, our imaginary school was no ordinary school and it had no ordinary headmistress. We were in a boarding school which the Head ran as a very tight ship. This may have been a reflection on the fact that we were by nature very messy and underneath we craved order. [I always thought of myself as a lazy perfectionist. Still do – Moo]. Inventing a strict headmistress at a boarding school gave us the boundaries we felt we needed. Beds made, rooms tidied, homework done – then the Head would come in to do an inspection. As the two of us represented the entire student population, the whole of the staff and a *very* critical Headteacher, it was necessary for Moo to switch roles and transform from a pupil into the Head. She rejoiced in the name of E. B. Speckle [goodness knows where we got that name from]. This was a satisfying role for Moo because she could indulge her tendency to nitpick and find fault. She could always find something really small to complain about. Her catch phrase was; '*All is not perfect!*' Saggy enjoyed the satisfying role of someone who took no notice of bossy people.

In our games we often gave ourselves other names. Usually Moo was 'Mary French' and Saggy was 'Anne French', although we do remember one of us being called 'Moona Lastic-Lips.

Bedtimes

You hear a lot among parents of young children about bedtimes. Should they have set bedtimes at all? And if they do, how do you get them to stay there if they don't want to? When we were children our mum expected us to be in bed quite early. So keen was she on this that she sometimes went to great lengths to get us there and make sure we stayed there. In my opinion, she was a pioneer in this field. You had to admire her ingenuity and persistence.

~

Bedtimes in our house could be fun. The first stage would involve Mum encouraging us up the stairs by terrifying the life out of us, chasing us and going *'Whoop! Whoop! Whoop!'* behind us, making pecking gestures with her hands. If she caught you, you would get a pinch on the bottom, but you never got caught because you got up those stairs in double quick time. Which, of course, was the whole idea.

The Bong Song

The next stage, getting undressed and ready for bed, was considerably enlivened by what we thought of as the Bong Song. Not a song really, but part of a poem Mum had learnt as a child and now scared us into bed with. It was about the curfew introduced by King William I to keep the peasants from revolt, and it went like this:

> *At bong number one they all started to run*
> *Like a warren of rabbits upset by a gun.*
> *At bong number two they were all in a stew*
> *Flinging cap after tunic and hose after shoe.*

Saggy & Moo

At bong number three they were bare to the knee
Undoing the doings as quick as could be.
At bong number four they were stripped to the core
Pulling on nightshirts the wrong side before.
At bong number five they were looking alive
Bizzing and buzzing like bees in a hive
At bong number six they gave themselves kicks
Tripping over rushes to snuff out the wicks
At bong number seven from Durham to Devon
They slipped up a prayer to our Father in heaven
At bong number eight they were all in a state
And with hearts beating all at a terrible rate
They jumped BONG into bed like a bull at a gate.

The pace and volume at which Mum delivered this verse started quite slow and quiet, and gradually picked up as it went along, finishing in a crescendo of terror with the final BONG, by which time you had better be in your bed or goodness knows what might happen to you.

~

If we were lucky, Mum might decide to have a bath when she had settled us into bed. On these occasions she would sing us lullabies and other soothing songs while she relaxed, hoping we'd drift contentedly off to sleep. It usually worked. You can't beat the sound of *'Scarlet Ribbons'* drifting steamily out of the bathroom to get you in the mood for sleep.

~

In summer we still had to go to bed at our bedtime, however light it might be outside. Mum would try to fool us into sleep by pegging a blanket over the curtains to make it dark, but it just

Inspiration and Elbow Grease

made it stuffy. Anyhow, we could still hear the enticing sounds of the summer evening going on outside – perhaps a neighbour mowing his lawn with a push- mower. A relaxing sound but not relaxing enough when you can also hear the sounds of other children playing. Lucky them, allowed to stay up and enjoy the balmy weather outside. Neighbours chatting and laughing, everyone happy and still enjoying the day while we had to be cooped up in a darkened room.

∼

So, did we drift off to sleep?

Of course not. We invented all sorts of ways to amuse ourselves. It was *just not possible* to resist the urge to peek behind the blanket and look at the world outside the window. Sometimes we would see the next door neighbour pottering about in his garden. On one occasion we thought we would shout things out of the window at him. It was so funny to imagine him glancing round nervously, wondering where on earth the voices were coming from. It hadn't dawned on us that he would know immediately. Anyhow, it seemed like a good idea at the time.

"Oi!" bawled Saggy: "YOU!"

"YOU DOWN THERE! YOU WITH THE BEARD!"

And we both disappeared double quick behind the blanket, pleased with ourselves and giggling uncontrollably. However, we had forgotten that he wasn't the only one who could hear us. All the neighbours who happened to be enjoying the evening sun also heard.

Unfortunately for us that included our parents. We only did it once.

Trying to get around the room without touching the floor was a favourite, but tended to get noisier than we meant it to. We might try sneaking across the landing to Squidge's room. That was dangerous, as you might get caught the wrong side of the top of the stairs. Usually, Mum would come up the stairs and tell us to be quiet. So we would subside for a few minutes before starting to chatter and giggle, getting louder without realising it. Mum would come toiling up the stairs again, getting a bit fed up now. And this would be repeated a few times, Mum starting to get really cheesed off. Then at last would come the ultimate chilling threat, the last resort of a mother whose patience was exhausted…

'If you don't stop it *Dad will be coming up…*'

We couldn't seem to help ourselves though and would be in the middle of larking about and giggling when we would become aware that Dad had materialised in the doorway. How long he had been there and how much he had heard we had no idea.

Anyway, that was the end of the naughtiness.

You didn't mess with Dad.

Story Time

When we were young, we had no alternative at night-time to having a book read to us. There were no story cassette tapes in the early 60s, no CDs for Mum to switch on and leave us to it, no iPad etc. She had to physically sit with us and turn the pages as she read to us and that is a different experience than listening to a tape. This was something we carried into the next generation.

Story Time was the highlight of the day for our own little ones. It was also enjoyed by the bigger ones. Often the routine went like this:

Inspiration and Elbow Grease

- After tea was cleared away, read to the little ones
- Put the little ones to bed
- Read to the middle kids
- Put the middle kids to bed
- Read to the teenagers
- Be bribed by the teenagers with cups of tea to read some more
- Put self to bed

Yes, it's true Mums are busier now, they go to work and have so many tasks set by primary schools these days from spelling tests, to reading books, to times tables, to projects and book days. But every now and then, snuggling down with your kids and reading to them is magical.

Just let them do it...

One of the things our kids most liked to do was make dens. One morning they constructed a particularly complicated one. I think there was a sofa inside it somewhere, and it looked like they had taken a cot apart for roof struts. They seemed to have purloined every single quilt, blanket and cushion in the house – but it was a *very quiet* morning for me.

Any remembrance of the process of clearing the whole thing up at the end of the day has been lost in the mists of time, but I'm sure I made them do it at some point. Though in the summer hols it was just so much easier to leave it there…

And another thing. Jumping in puddles. Why stop them? They will do it anyway. I started off saying 'Don't jump in the puddles' just because my Mum said it to me, and OK on the way to school is not a good time. But why not let them do it on the way home and give them clean socks in the morning, if they have some. It would save so much nervous energy if we didn't automatically keep stopping them doing stuff that isn't dangerous, but just inconvenient.

Kids love taking things apart, which is fine as long as you don't expect them to put them back together. Just give 'em an old radio or laptop and a screwdriver and leave them alone. We also found that children will play happily for hours with play dough, which is cheap and easily made at home from flour and salt.

Recipe for play dough

Mix together in a bowl:

- 2 cups flour [these are American ones]
- 2 tbsp Alum [we used cream of tartar]
- Heat to boiling:
- 1½, cups water
- Half cup salt
- 1 tbsp oil
- Food colouring

Stir liquids into dry ingredients. Knead until smooth. Store into an airtight container.

[*More With Less Cookbook*. Doris Longacre]

Don't tell your mother

Some of the best fun our children had was while we weren't looking and didn't find out about until years later.

My children used to climb out of the upstairs bathroom window, drop down onto the lean-to roof and somehow get down to the ground and out into the garden. How did I not notice this?

However, the thing that really makes me come out in a cold sweat is the suite of underground rooms and tunnels they constructed. I can only assume they have exaggerated this story. I mean, I knew they were digging a couple of holes in the garden, that was all. Or so I thought. Apparently, it was all done properly, reinforced and all that, but it surely can't have been safe. They could have been buried alive! Eventually they were rumbled when their dad noticed the tunnel entrance and put a stop to the whole thing. I suspect it was a case of 'don't tell your mother' in case I had a hairy fit. I was told they had been trying to make a tunnel but had been made to fill it in. I didn't find out the extent of the excavations until many years later when all danger of hairy fits had passed.

I used to let the boys go out to play in the fields near where we lived. I knew they had a wonderful time out in the fresh air and sunshine and came home happy although maybe a little grubby and damp. What I didn't know until recently is that they had been riding down the river on home-made rafts.

The children discovered a place in our large garden where a small person could squeeze, unseen from the house, into a neighbour's garden. I didn't know about this until the neighbour turned up on our doorstep with a grubby toddler who was wearing a cheeky grin, a T shirt, and nothing else.

'Is this one of yours?' she asked. What could I say? Naturally it was one of ours, no point in denying it.

Children don't need a lot of stuff. When they have too much stuff, they get confused and just pour the toys all over the floor and then go outside to play in the dirt with a spoon.

Kate Singh

Days Out

We all enjoyed days out as a family. Maybe not Alton Towers or anywhere like that en masse. Our outings tended to be based on economical lines, avoiding any per head entrance fees if possible. Going to the beach was always a favourite but, to avoid the worst of the heat, the crowds and opportunities for children getting lost, we often went in the late afternoon when other families were starting to head home. That way we'd find it easier to get a parking space and had a bit more room to spread ourselves out.

We were a sea-loving family, so perhaps it wasn't surprising that eventually we should acquire a boat or two. Now, families the size of ours don't often manage to run to a boat, so it's not surprising that the ones we had weren't exactly flashy or large. First, we acquired a lovingly restored but antiquated wooden sailing dinghy. Then a dear old boat that went by the unflattering but appropriate name of *The Barnacle*. She was a heavy but lovable old girl. After adding a new engine, she was ready to go, although she was never going to break any speed records or win a beauty contest. But we loved her.

Inspiration and Elbow Grease

One fine day it was decided to give the dinghy her first outing in the sea. Our eldest girl, who had recently got an NVQ in sailing, would be the skipper, taking a couple of other girls with her. My husband, known to the Harbourmaster as 'Barnacle Bill' for obvious reasons, but never addressed as such to his face for equally obvious reasons, would naturally captain *The Barnacle*. He would keep an eye on the girls to make sure they were ok.

As the crews were getting their boats afloat, they couldn't help but notice a flashy bright yellow speed boat that was swanking about back and forth across the bay. Her name was *'The Flying Banana'*. At least if it wasn't, it should have been. Much as the kids loved *The Barnacle*, it was hard not to be just a teensy bit envious. What wouldn't they give for a go in that!

Anyhow, off they sailed and chugged together across the bay, all envy forgotten in the joy of being afloat. Sadly, for the crew of the dinghy, it didn't last long.

"DON'T GO TOO CLOSE TO THE BEACH", bawled the captain of *The Barnacle* to the girls in the dinghy.

"WE WON'T", they bawled back. And then did.

The dinghy bumped its bottom on the beach, but they managed to get it back out to sea a little way. It soon became obvious that the boat was filling with water. The self-baler had been damaged and a hole had been knocked in the bottom.

"DAD! WE'RE SINKING!" yelled the girls.

"NO, YOU'RE NOT" yelled back Dad.

"YES, WE ARE!"

"YOU WON'T SINK. JUST BAIL OUT THE WATER."

"WE *ARE* BAILING IT OUT. AND WE *ARE* SINKING."

"NO, YOU AREN'T SINKING!"

Saggy & Moo

"WE ARE!!" They yelled. And did.

The dinghy turned turtle and all the girls ended up in the water. This wasn't the unmitigated disaster it might have been because of two things.

Firstly, *The Flying Banana* stopped swanking about across the bay and came to the rescue. The girls were heaved aboard and got the ride of their dreams back to the harbour.

Secondly, Dad did a superhero leap over the side of The *Barnacle* and after a struggle managed to free the mast of the dinghy which had become trapped in some rocks. The harbourmaster and every tourist in town were lined up along the harbour, laughing their socks off as they videoed it all.

All's well that ends well, as they say. Nobody drowned, but sadly that was the end of the dinghy.

∽

There was only one occasion when we took both our families to the beach together when the children were all young, thinking what fun it would be for them to have each other to play with. And it was, but not surprisingly we found ourselves mistaken for a Sunday school outing. Keeping an accurate head count was even more complicated than usual and I don't know how we managed to return with the same number of children we left home with.

Another source of free entertainment was a stretch of common land up in the local hills known to the family as Mini Moor, where the children could run around. But the best thing about it was a huge old tree which had a rope swing hanging from its branches. The kids and their dad spent many a happy hour there while I spent happy hours at home supposedly catching up on my many outstanding jobs but, in reality, drinking tea and enjoying a rare interval of peace and quiet.

Waiting With Style

Because there were so many children in the family, we always seemed to be attending one appointment or another. It felt like I spent half my life in waiting rooms.

Now, in order to get the most out of these boring and/or stressful occasions, and to stop me wasting half my life, we had to find a way to liven them up a bit. Being blessed with lively and imaginative kids who were always up for a laugh, we usually managed to squeeze a fair bit of fun out of just waiting. We called it waiting with style.

For example, I once had to take six of the brood for dental check-ups. In order to make it less stressful [nobody likes going to the dentist, even for check-ups] we pretended that the clinic was a prison, the nurses and receptionists were the guards, a role for which they seemed to be eminently suited, and the surgery/dentists lair was obviously the torture chamber. The kids took turns in doing reconnaissance [going to the toilet] to spy out the lie of the land so we could plan our escape. There was a lot of whispering between prisoners, passing on of information vital to our escape.

As each prisoner was carted off for their turn in the torture chamber in the custody of a grim guard, they were cheered on their way with words of encouragement by the others. The victim would return some minutes later, declaring to a mildly alarmed waiting room that the inquisitor hadn't been able to get anything out of them, despite all the ghastly torture equipment at his disposal.

Eventually everyone had had their turn under torture, and when all were returned to the custody of the waiting room, I distracted the guards [made any necessary appointments for treatment] while the kids made good their escape. Once we were all in the getaway car, there was an exciting dash across town while the escapees kept an eye out for anyone following us. Phew, they hadn't missed us yet. There had been talk of leaving dummies in our seats to fool the guards, but that idea was obviously never going to work.

I'd like to present myself as the frazzled martyr struggling to cope, but I have to admit I enjoyed it as much as the kids. Anyway, I can't be sure it wasn't my idea in the first place. And as the kids weren't noisy or disruptive, nobody else was inconvenienced. In fact, that was the best part – it kept the kids reasonably quiet as well as entertained.

The Grandma who turned Socks into Rabbits

Following their unconventional approach to parenting and family life, our Mum and Dad carried over their unique take on life into grandparenting. Basically, they made it up as they went

Inspiration and Elbow Grease

along. You could never be sure what they'd do next. I suppose Saggy and I should have known better when our Mum offered to fetch our primary school children home one day when she was visiting us. This was at the time when our two families lived next door to each other, and we had racked up a fair number of kids between us. So, off Grandma went to the school with a length of rope concealed about her person. She wasn't leaving anything to chance.

When Grandma had rounded up the correct number of children (just nine of them at the time) and checked that she'd got the right ones, she produced the rope and corralled the kids inside it. Off home she set with them all roped together, down the street and across the roads getting the sort of funny looks she was well used to and happily ignoring them all. The kids thought it was great. Nobody else had a Grandma who was quite so much fun.

Grandma never came to visit without helping out somehow, most often by sorting out and pairing up odd socks. This wasn't such an easy job as it sounds, which is why I hadn't usually got around to it myself. It was sock chaos and Grandma loved it; it was right up her street.

As the children got bigger and the family grew, the number of socks increased until they seemed to be everywhere, clean and dirty. Grandma came into this mayhem like Wonder-Woman and heroically brought order. I would produce a mountain of clean socks and she would settle herself down to tackle it, fortified with occasional cups of tea, until at last there was a pile of paired socks all done up like little rabbits and an almost as large pile of socks for which no partner could be found.

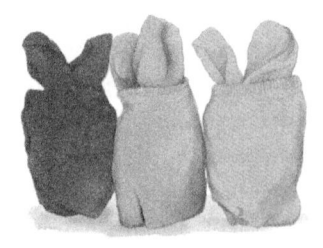

The Grandfather who Numbered Eggs

It slowly dawned on us that our parents weren't quite the same as everybody else's when we used to swap stories with our friends of what we did in the holidays or at the weekend. Nobody else we knew had parents that lay in a circle on the living room floor with Mum's head resting on Dad's stomach as a pillow, one sister's head on Mum's tummy, another sister's head resting on the first sister's tummy, and our little brother's head resting on the last sister. And there we would lay, in the dark of an evening, telly off, just talking.

We soon stopped telling people that we only went to the seaside in the winter specifically because *nobody else was there*, or that we developed a list of unusually named trusses for men with hernias. We used to think that when we grew up we wouldn't think that our parents were as weird as they seemed to others at the time, or that we would perhaps find out that other people's parents also did odd things.

But no. Our friends' parents were civil servants and tax officials who had dinner parties and drank wine. Their Mums wore aprons and did housework. Our Mum didn't think much of housework, she preferred to sing us funny songs when she had a bath, her voice drifting across the landing at night to our bedrooms singing three children to bed at once. Or gardening. Or even cleaning out drains.

Inspiration and Elbow Grease

But as they both aged and we both moved to the other end of the country [these two facts are not related] we saw our parents less and less and assumed that they had grown up at last and had become more normal. We also hoped that our father would behave himself in a mature manner on formal occasions.

We were mistaken:

The day finally came when they moved West to be near us so we could once again keep an eye on them. Apart from our Mum's habit of saying the rude things to people that normally people only *think* but don't *say* and our Dad's habit of drawing cartoons of two words that make a funny picture [you have to see it really], we thought we were home and dry.

Then this happened:

He would take eggs home, and unable to place complete confidence in the date stamp on the egg box within which his eggs are placed, he would carefully take each egg out and write the date on the shell. He didn't just scribble the number on with any old biro or use the pencil he keeps behind his ear which is useful for crosswords. No, he got out a superior marker pen and printed the numbers in a perfect script as if they will be photographed for posterity [which they have been].

This was understandable at least from a perishable point of view, but then he moved on to margarine tubs. With margarine tubs, I think he realised that the date stamp on the tubs could be trusted, [margarine is indestructible] but *how many had they opened in total since they moved in?* This was obviously a question he felt that needed to be answered. The problem preyed on his mind. These tubs should be numbered so that they could be progressed through in an orderly fashion, and they could also see how many they had used. But, eighty three? We were only slightly more concerned about his state of mind, than the sheer volume of synthetic butter he had consumed…

Some of Dad's doodles.

Inspiration and Elbow Grease

I rest my case...

We had to become resigned to the fact that we had ever so slightly weird parents and we should have stopped trying to hide them from the outside world. After all, something must be right judging from a comment passed by an old neighbour when all us kids were still living at home:

'You could often hear laughter coming from your house. You seemed to be having such a good time.'

Oh, we were...

Where Are We Now?

In our 60s for one thing…

Actually busier than when we had children. Except we can more or less do what we want, when we want. Which, as parents will know, is not possible when you still have kids at home.

It's been fun looking back at those busy years of mothering and homemaking. Although it hasn't all been plain sailing, we have had so many good times, so many laughs, so much fun along the way. Now we have more time, which is just as well because everything seems to take longer now we are older.

For years we looked forward to a time when we could wake naturally in the morning, have a leisurely shower and relaxed breakfast before starting the business of the day.

Guys! The day has come! We can sit in our beds with a cup of tea [and sometimes a laptop or iPad] listening to the birds singing and mulling over what we will do each day. We can have a shower without anybody banging on the door wanting help with finding school books, or hearing the baby crying for a bottle. We look at the weather forecast and plan a walk, or work in the

Where Are We Now?

garden knowing there is no school run to fit in. Life is at such a slower pace we can hardly believe how busy we once were. Now we are busy in a different way, and it is good.

Grandchildren have entered our lives [47 between us] which have brought us such joy and pleasure. We look on with interest while our children deal with some o the same issues that we had to deal with, and some new ones [like internet use] which we didn't.

Our mother is now nearly 94 and still entertaining us with stories of her past, and looking on with interest while we in turn deal with some of the issues that she has had to deal with as we have grown old.

There is so much we haven't included in this book. We keep thinking of things to say, things we've only just remembered. We have had a good time remembering and laughing over our shared past and experiences, as sisters often do. And we do hope our long-suffering brother doesn't mind being referred to as Squidge.

Appendix

Here you will find resources that we both used as young mums, some were used up until the present day, and some are new. We didn't use all of them all the time, some we went back to, and some we discovered recently and included in our lives. As people we are all shaped by many different inputs, and over time, we discover what suits us best. These resources may help you, they may not. You may find them frustrating, laughable, out of touch, or just what you need.

Websites

Hodmedod's: Britain's Pulse & Grain Pioneers
Do you need organic gluten-free flour that's not using rice or potatoes?
Would you like to find a British firm that is producing high-quality alternatives to highly-priced white gluten-free flours…
Hodmedod's is a firm you should get acquainted with if you want to, or need to, go gluten-free. They have a big range of alternative flours made from dried peas, broad beans and quinoa, and stuff like bean and barley ferments. The flours are

the reason I was interested in the firm, but then I got drawn in to their unusual pulses, and then I got drawn in to their vast array of recipes…
This is the list that comes up under the recipe tab:
I used the yellow pea flour the make a savoury pancake for when I need a bit of stodge, but want to avoid bread /rice/potatoes. If I make the batter thin it's a pancake, if I make it thick it is like a flatbread base on which I put fried onions, mushrooms and courgettes to which I have added either red or green pesto.
And, I can make the batter with just water; no eggs or milk needed if you don't want them, or haven't got them.
Nick Saltmarsh, Josiah Meldrum and William Hudson founded Hodmedod's in 2012 to supply beans and other products from British farms. They work with British farms to source a range of top quality ingredients and delicious foods. And have introduced less well-known foods, like the fava bean – grown in Britain since the Iron Age but now almost forgotten – and black badger peas. Their aim was to stimulate and assess demand for indigenous pulses.
https://hodmedods.co.uk/

Sharpham Park: our local organically grown spelt flour…
I made the decision to buy spelt flour because, as an ancient grain, I understood that the gluten molecule in spelt didn't irritate the gut as much as the gluten molecule in modern wheat flour. The molecular shape had been altered after tinkering in the lab to produce a grain that didn't grow so high that is was bowed down by the heavy head when ripe, or blown over in high winds; a grain that wasn't stunted so that it could be scooped up efficiently by the grain harvester, a grain that was resistant to pests and diseases, and that ripened at the right time. Apparently all these changes impacted on the final structure of the gluten molecule to make it harder for the human gastrointestinal system to digest.

Appendix

And I wanted *organic* spelt.
At the back of my mind somewhere I wondered if I was being too picky. I wondered if I should be searching the UK high and low for the perfect flour to suit my needs when I could always go to Sainsbury's and pick up flour they sourced from somewhere or other.
But then I found Sharpham Park: flour millers that produced the organic spelt I was looking for, and they were located in my county. I could almost drive over and pick it up...
I buy boxes of the stuff at a time. And I love the Union Flag on the boxes. I love the nearness of it, the localness.
Not everybody has flour grown in their home county, but we all have something near us. Find out what your thing is and support it...
https://www.sharphampark.com/

Books

How do you find the time? [Pat King]
'How to have all the time you need – every day'.
How to Win at Housework [Don Aslett]
'Solutions to the 100 most common and most awkward household problems.'
Is There Life After Housework? [Don Aslett]
'A revolutionary approach to free you from the drudgery of housework.'
Cheaper by the Dozen
[not strictly *helpful* in a practical way. Read the book, the film is an embarrassment]
Pauper's Cookbook [Jocasta Innes]
'Jocasta Innes dreamed of a cookery book planned for Church mice.'
More with Less Cook Book [Doris Longacre]
'How to eat better and consume less of the world's resources.'
Let's Cook it Right [Adelle Davis]
Let's Have Healthy Children [Adelle Davis}

Appendix

This woman was a pioneer in nutrition, way ahead of her time…
<u>Superwoman [Shirley Conran]</u>
'Cheerful & friendly, sensible & practical, this is a guide to saving stress, time and money.'
<u>Modern Vegetarian Cookery [Walter and Jenny Fliess]</u>
The origins of Baked Savoury Roll…
<u>Little House in the Big Woods [Laura Ingalls Wilder]</u>
We read the whole series to our kids at bedtime. Several times over…
<u>The Homemade Housewife</u> [Kate Singh]

Printed in Great Britain
by Amazon